SO-AVM-681

The Life of the Church

LAYMAN'S LIBRARY OF CHRISTIAN DOCTRINE

The Life of the Church
LAVONN D. BROWN

BROADMAN PRESS
Nashville, Tennessee

© Copyright 1987 • Broadman Press

All rights reserved

4216-43

ISBN: 0-8054-1643-9

Dewey Decimal Classification: 262

Subject Heading: CHURCH

Library of Congress Catalog Card Number: 86-23269

Printed in the United States of America

Unless otherwise noted, Scripture quotations are from the Revised Standard Version of the Bible, copyrighted 1946, 1952, © 1971, 1973.

Scripture quotations marked (ASV) are from the American Standard Version of the Bible.

Scripture quotations marked (KJV) are from the King James Version of the Bible.

Library of Congress Cataloging-in-Publication Data

Brown, Lavonn D.
   The life of the church.

   (Layman's library of Christian doctrine; 13)
   Includes index.
   1. Church.   2 Southern Baptist Convention—Doctrines.
3. Baptists—Doctrines.   I. Title.   II. Series.
BV600.2.B724   1987   262   86-23269
ISBN 0-8054-1643-9

To Norma
My wife, companion, challenge, inspiration
and to Matthew
My first grandson

and acknowledgment
for Ginger Geis
who faithfully and accurately typed the manuscript

Foreword

The *Layman's Library of Christian Doctrine* in sixteen volumes covers the major doctrines of the Christian faith.

To meet the needs of the lay reader, the *Library* is written in a popular style. Headings are used in each volume to help the reader understand which part of the doctrine is being dealt with. Technical terms, if necessary to the discussion, will be clearly defined.

The need for this series is evident. Christians need to have a theology of their own, not one handed to them by someone else. The *Library* is written to help readers evaluate and form their own beliefs based on the Bible and on clear and persuasive statements of historic Christian positions. The aim of the series is to help laymen hammer out their own personal theology.

The books range in size from 140 pages to 168 pages. Each volume deals with a major part of Christian doctrine. Although some overlap is unavoidable, each volume will stand on its own. A set of the sixteen-volume series will give a person a complete look at the major doctrines of the Christian church.

Each volume is personalized by its author. The author will show the vitality of Christian doctrines and their meaning for everyday life. Strong and fresh illustrations will hold the interest of the reader. At times the personal faith of the authors will be seen in illustrations from their own Christian pilgrimage.

Not all laymen are aware they are theologians. Many may believe they know nothing of theology. However, every person believes something. This series helps the layman to understand what he believes and to be able to be "prepared to make a defense to any one who calls [him] to account for the hope that is in [him]" (1 Pet. 3:15, RSV).

Contents

Contents

Part I
The Church:
A Caring Community

1

A Fellowship of Loving Concern

We have never understood the church. Perhaps, we never will. Some things about the church we consider vital, essential, irreplaceable. Others we consider unnecessary, boring, detrimental. What are our alternatives? Not so good.

The mental images produced by the word *church* are as varied as they are partial. Choose one or more of the following: The church is

—a congregation of saints having achieved varying levels of sinless perfection

—a fellowship of sinners banded together to help each other live a better life

—a museum for collecting and preserving holy relics

—a spiritual army marching off the map with divine commands

—a house of hypocrisy where people play games with God

—a fellowship of loving concern picking up broken lives and restoring them.

Ken Medema, the blind musician, often sees more than those of us with good vision. He wrote a song about the church.

> I don't need another place
> for trying to impress you
> with just how good and virtuous I am.
>
> I don't need another place
> for always being on top of things,
> ev'rybody knows that it's a sham.

> I don't need another place
> for always wearing smiles,
> even when it's not the way I feel.

> I don't need another place
> to mouth the same old platitudes,
> You and I both know that it's not real.

Medema is searching for a church, a message, a ministry that has a ring of the real. He goes on to ask some pertinent questions:

> If this is not a place
> where tears are understood,
> where can I go to cry?

> And if this is not a place
> where my spirit can take wings,
> where can I go to fly?

> If this is not a place
> where my questions can be asked,
> where shall I go to seek?

> And if this is not a place
> where my heart cries can be heard,
> where shall I go to speak?[1]

Love means different things to different people. So does church. Many people think of church in terms of a building. It is located at the corner of Webster and Comanche. Therefore, one says, "We are building a new church." Others think of church as a particular denomination, as in, "To which church do you belong?" The expected answer would include Presbyterian, Baptist, or Roman Catholic.

The word *church* may be used of an institution. In the 1960s, university students were chanting "Jesus, yes. Church, no " They held little hope for the institutional church. Asked what he thought of the church, a student replied, "Not much! It doesn't scratch where I itch!" Sometimes the church means nothing more than a worship service, as in, "Are you going to church Sunday?"

The danger is not that these concepts are wrong or evil. Rather, it is that they are partial and inadequate. The question is, What would Christ have the church to be? Or, become?

Ken Medema would insist that the church should be a place of mutual forgiveness and mutual concern. It should be a place where each member gives priority to the others' need. It must be a fellowship of loving concern.

What is the *church*? Technically the word refers to those who have been "called out." Years ago I memorized a definition of church for my ordination service. I still find satisfaction in it. Simply, yet comprehensively, the church is "a body of baptized believers bound together voluntarily to carry out Christ's divine commission to disciple, baptize, and teach" (see Matt. 28:19-20).

The Origin of the Church

It is difficult to designate any particular time or place as the day of the church's birth or origin. Some scholars even deny that Jesus intended to form a community. Yet, the evidence leaves little doubt that Jesus foresaw a community of believing people built together by a common faith in Him. (In volume 12 of the "Layman's Library of Christian Doctrine," *The Nature of the Church*, Bill Leonard deals with this topic at length.)

Church Roots in the Old Testament

The church, like many other New Testament concepts, has its roots in the Old Testament. The relationship between Yahweh and the congregation of Israel prefigures the relationship between Christ and His disciples. When the Israelites were delivered from bondage, they became "the called-out ones." God dealt with people in community. Israel was considered "holy" unto the Lord. That meant that her people were separate to Yahweh and separate from the value systems of the world.

The early church looked to a definite and distinct background in the history recorded in the Old Testament. The Bible is a book about God's relationship with His people. The Jews were God's chosen people. They were chosen not for special privilege but for special responsibility. God entered into an agreement, or covenant relationship with them. A major theme in the Old Testament is the faithfulness of God and the faithlessness of His people. Israel failed to live up to her part of the agreement.

The Congregation of Israel and the Christian Community

When Christ came, a remnant within Israel first believed in Him. The early Christian community looked upon itself as a continuation of the Old Testament people of God. At first the Christian community saw no reason to discontinue its Jewish connections. The disciples of Jesus formed an open fellowship within Israel.

Gradually the Jews failed to fulfill their special responsibility. Their prophetic note was lost. In so doing, they disqualified themselves as the true people of God. The Christian community began a slow process of moving away from its Jewish associations.

The Church Came from Christ

The church can never be understood apart from Jesus Christ. The church is the new creation of Christ Himself. The growth of the church was from Christian fellowship to organized institution.

The exact beginning of the church is not easy to determine. It is like asking when an oak tree began. Did it begin with an acorn, the root system, a visible sprout, or a full-grown tree?[2] The important thing is not determining the church's precise beginning but the fact that it does exist.

Jesus personally called a group of disciples. They became the embryo of a new community. When the twelve apostles sat down with Jesus in the upper room, they became a nucleus of the church. When He said, "On this rock I will build my church" (Matt. 16:18), He obviously intended the formation of a fellowship group which embodies the idea of the church.

However, the church did not begin to take form until after the death and resurrection of Christ. In the strictest sense, the church was created by the good news. As soon as people gathered together through faith in the resurrection of the crucified Jesus of Nazareth, the church came into existence. The church was and is the community of the risen Lord.

What About Pentecost?

The church as Christian fellowship was in existence before Pentecost. However, many Christians trace the origin of the church as a self-conscious community to that thrilling event described in Acts 2. God, the Holy Spirit, manifested Himself in peoples' lives as transforming power. The abiding presence of the Holy Spirit is a continuing source of vitality and courage for the church. The living presence of the risen Christ rests upon the entire company not a select few.

The church cannot be understood apart from the activity of the Holy Spirit. Following Pentecost a more self-conscious group emerged, and those who were being baptized were added to the group (Acts 2:41). Pentecost was the critical event which launched the church's worldwide mission. On that day the church was empowered for its mission.

R. Newton Flew, in *Jesus and His Church*, made this summary statement:

> It [the church] is old in the sense that it is a continuation of the life of Israel, the People of God. It is new in the sense that it is founded on the revelation made through Jesus Christ of God's final purpose for mankind.[3]

The Nature of the Church

"Let the church be the church" is an oft-heard plea. But what is the church? If you decided to destroy your church, what would you do? Would you set fire to the building? Tear out the baptistry? Burn all the budgets?

The word *church* is used in the New Testament with a twofold meaning. In some instances, it refers to the whole body of believers, the fellowship of the redeemed everywhere, the people of God assembled or unassembled. In most cases, however, church refers to a local congregation. So, the Lord Jesus is head of the church composed of all true believers. At the same time, Christians are to associate themselves into particular local congregations of churches. Therefore, local congregations share the nature of the body of Christ.

What did Jesus mean by *ekklēsia* (church)? At the time of Peter's great confession, Jesus said, "And on this rock I will build my church" (Matt. 16:18). Later, while discussing church discipline, He said, "If he refuses to listen to them, tell it to the church" (Matt. 18:17). The word *church* literally means the called-out ones or those who have been summoned together. When Jesus used the word *church,* He was referring to a group of people whom He had called to be with Him in special relationship. Early Christians first used the word to describe simple meetings and later to describe local congregations.

Paul S. Minear in his *Images of the Church in the New Testament* lists ninety-six terms used to describe the church in the New Testament. Three of these analogies help us understand the special relationship of the church to God as Father, Son, and Holy Spirit.

The Church as "the People of God"

What will be the relationship between the church and God the Father? In the Old Testament, the Israelites were the people of God. The early Christian community saw itself as a continuation of the new Israel to evangelize all nations. This concept placed the New Testament church in the setting of the long story of God's dealings with His chosen people. "The people of God" may be the best term to describe the nature of the New Testament church.

Peter described "the exiles of the Dispersion" (1 Pet. 1:1) in this way:

> But you are a chosen race, a royal priesthood, a holy nation, God's own people, that you may declare the wonderful deeds of him who

called you out of darkness into his marvelous light. Once you were no people but now you are God's people; once you had not received mercy but now you have received mercy (1 Pet. 2:9-10).

Paul sought to justify taking the gospel to the Gentiles by quoting the prophet Hosea:

Those who were not my people I will call "my people," and her who was not beloved I will call "my beloved." And in the very place where it was said to them, "You are not my people," they will be called "sons of the living God" (Rom. 9:25-26).

The church is essentially a people, a religious society. It is not a building, but the believers themselves. The claim to be the people of God is not an arbitrary claim to special privilege. It should not lead to pride but to repentance. The church is the people of God only because He dwells within and moves among His people.

As the people of God, the church must embody the good news in everyday life. Since God has forgiven, the people of God must forgive. Since God has loved, the people of God must love. The people of God must forever be a missionary and evangelizing people, taking the gospel to all people and nations.

The Church as "the Body of Christ"

The relationship between Jesus Christ and the church is best understood in Paul's metaphor of the body of Christ. Paul spoke out of conviction when he said to the Corinthians, "Now you are the body of Christ and individually members of it" (1 Cor. 12:27). The concept has tremendous potential.

Unity in diversity is the best we can hope for in the church. Paul wanted us to understand that "just as the body is one [unity] and has many members [diversity], and all the members of the body, though many [diversity], are one body [unity], so it is with Christ. For the body does not consist of one member [unity], but of many [diversity]" (1 Cor. 12:12,14).

In the mind of New Testament Christians, Christ and the church were inseparable realities. Christ did not leave merely changed, isolated individuals. He left a body of believers, the church. To think of Christ is necessarily to think of the church. To think of the church is necessarily to think of Christ. The work of the church is Christ's work. Through the church, His purposes are carried out in the world.

In the church, each person is not only a member of the body of Christ but also a member of all the other Christians who make up the body. "For as in one body we have many members," Paul wrote, "and all the members do not have the same function, so we, though many, are one body in Christ, and individually members of one another" (Rom. 12:4-5).

The members are so bound together that each person feels keenly the hurts, sorrows, and joys that come to the rest of the family. Paul urged "that there may be no discord in the body, but that the members may have the same care for one another. If one member suffers, all suffer together; if one member is honored, all rejoice together" (1 Cor. 12:25-26).

The head of the body is Christ. Paul reminded the Colossians, "He is the head of the body, the church; he is the beginning, the first-born from the dead, that in everything he might be pre-eminent" (Col. 1:18). The church is a new creation in Him, and it partakes of the very life of Christ. The church's reason for being is to minister to the world as Christ's agent.

The Church as "the Fellowship of the Spirit"

The church also has a vital relationship to the person and work of the Holy Spirit. In fact, the church cannot be understood apart from the activity of the Holy Spirit. The book in the New Testament called "The Acts of the Apostles" may be more accurately named "The Acts of the Holy Spirit."

On the day of Pentecost, the Holy Spirit manifested Himself in people's lives as a transforming power. The Holy Spirit is best understood as the living presence of the risen Christ. One of the favorite descriptions of the church in the New Testament was fellowship *(koinōnia)*. Paul closed his letter to the Corinthian church with the familiar benediction referring to "the fellowship of the Holy Spirit" (2 Cor. 13:14). This fellowship of loving concern was a product of the Spirit's presence.[4]

The Necessity of the Church

Do you agree or disagree with this statement: "You don't need to go to church to be a good Christian"? If you agree, you belong to a majority of American church members. What about this statement attributed to John Wesley: "There is no such thing as a solitary Christian"? Agree or disagree?

Is the church necessary for the Christian life? Opinions vary greatly. Some see no salvation apart from the church. Others see no hope of salvation within the church. Where did the idea of the church come from anyway?

The Desire for Community

We experience fully what it means to be human beings only in community with other people. Modern psychology places much emphasis on the universal desire for community. People dislike isolation, aloneness, alienation. The isolation of death row is an extreme form of punishment.

People want to belong. They band together in all kinds of groups and organizations, both good and bad, in order to experience community. The group may be Boy Scouts or a street gang. It may be a fraternal or civic organization. It may be a church or a home Bible study group. People either join existing communities or create new ones.

The Church Provides Community

The New Testament insists that conversion is the gateway leading to inclusion within a wider community. Every Christian needs the church; the church needs every Christian. Through the church, the Christian becomes a vital member of the body of Christ. He or she belongs. More than that, through the local community, the Christian is put in touch with the worldwide community.

The Christian message has reached us through other people. We depend on others both for our knowledge of Christ and our growth in Him. William Temple stressed the mutual dependence of Christian people when he said, "It is by the faith of others that our faith is kindled."[5]

The church, then is not external or incidental to the Christian life. Rather it belongs to the central realities of the believing life. Some people have concluded that to live a full-grown Christian life outside the fellowship of the Christian community is impossible. Christians will satisfy their need for belonging in one way or another. Those who bypass the church will seek out a substitute, either worthy or unworthy. Elton Trueblood concluded, "There can never be a Churchless Christianity."[6]

Entrance to the Church

Who should belong to the church? Who should constitute its membership?

Conversion, the First Essential

The gateway to inclusion in the church is conversion. The church's members are regenerated, transformed people who have met Christ face to face. Only those who give credible evidence that they have received Christ as Savior and Lord should be received into membership.

In the early church, "the Lord added to their number day by day those who were being saved" (Acts 2:47). The people had voluntarily "received his word" (v. 41), repented of their sins, and believed in Christ as Savior.

The church is a spiritual organization; it is the body of Christ. Entrance into the body of Christ is a spiritual experience. The work of the church is spiritual. Those who do this work must have spiritual discernment.

Baptism, a Public Profession

Baptism is the Christian's formal profession to the world. It is
the key to entrance to the local church. "So those who received
his word were baptized," Luke wrote, "and there were added that
day about three thousand souls" (Acts 2:41). Baptism is an expression of the new life found in Christ. It is a vital part of one's
public profession of faith in Christ. It is a testimony to one's death
to an old way of life without Christ, burial to the old way, and
resurrection to newness of life in Christ (Rom. 6:4).

Church Membership, a Voluntary Matter

Becoming a Christian is a voluntary matter. Baptism is a voluntary matter. Therefore, church membership is always a voluntary
matter. Every person must hear, repent, believe, be baptized, and
join the church for oneself. It must ever be a matter of personal
choice.

Understanding Fellowship (Koinōnia)

The church grew out of Christian fellowship. Believers, bound
together by their common love for Christ and one another, became
the church. Fellowship was one of the striking elements of the
early church. To early Christians it was inconceivable that a believer would go into isolation. To be a believer was to be a believer
in fellowship.

Koinōnia is fellowship with the triune God. Paul closed his letter to the Corinthian church with the familiar benediction: "The
grace of the Lord Jesus Christ and the love of God and the fellowship of the Holy Spirit be with you all" (2 Cor. 13:14). The fellowship level of any church, then or now, is vitally related to the
person and work of the Holy Spirit.

The presence of the Holy Spirit joins believers with the resur-
rected Jesus and makes possible their fellowship with one another.
The concept of fellowship is one of the significant ways in Scrip-

ture of expressing a central Christian mystery, the union in love of God and man through Jesus Christ.

The Biblical Development of the Idea

The Old Testament development.—There is no full understanding of *koinōnia* in the Old Testament. The writer of Ecclesiastes came close to the idea in this foregleam of fellowship:

> Two are better than one, because they have a good reward for their toil. For if they fall, one will lift up his fellow; but woe to him who is alone when he falls and he has not another to lift him up. Again, if two lie together, they are warm; but how can one be warm alone? And though a man might prevail against one who is alone, two will withstand him. A threefold cord is not quickly broken (4:9-12).

The equivalent Hebrew term for fellowship may have been used to describe the group of pietistic Jews known as the Pharisees. They saw themselves as "the separated ones," devoted to God and God's will.

The New Testament development.—The concept of fellowship emerged in the formative days of the church. Three thousand were converted, baptized, and added to the church on the Day of Pentecost. What did they do after Pentecost? Luke said, "They devoted themselves to the apostles' teaching and fellowship [*koinōnia*], to the breaking of bread and the prayers" (Acts 2:42). Love welded the people of highly diverse backgrounds and personalities into a genuine fellowship.

The apostles' teaching was composed of the witness and first-hand stories about Jesus preserved by those who knew Him. The breaking of bread may have referred to common meals, but probably included the observance of the Lord's Supper as commanded by Christ. The prayers included both the private and shared prayers of fellow believers.

The apostle's fellowship described the believers' common life together—a total sharing of life. This sense of fellowship expressed itself in a distinctive way. The Christian community was apparently made up of many poor people and widows who had no source of support. Those who shared the blessings of the messianic age were led to an actual sharing of possessions with those less fortunate. "All who believed were together and had all things in common; and they sold their possessions and goods and distributed them to all, as any had need" (Acts 2:44-45). Sharing of goods was strictly voluntary and arose out of a deep experience of divine love.

Voluntariness and love represent the crucial difference between the practice of the early church and the model of Marxist Communism. In Communism, the classless society and the equal distribution of goods comes at the end of a deliberate plan, not the beginning. In the beginning, the dictatorship of the proletariat must impose proper distribution until everyone recognizes mutual responsibility. It is not a voluntary system. In theory, the time will come when the dictatorship will cease and everyone will accept their responsibility to share. In fact, no Marxist dictatorship has ceased because the people willingly accepted their responsibility to share. Only divine love can create genuine fellowship and sharing.

An even higher expression of fellowship is found in the writings of Paul. In fact, *koinōnia* may be considered the ruling idea behind the first Corinthian letter. To that church, torn apart by party-groupings and divisiveness, Paul wrote, "God is faithful, by whom you were called into the fellowship of his Son, Jesus Christ our Lord" (1:9). Paul's call for unity was based on the common life shared by all believers. In his letter to the Philippian church, Paul thanked God for their "partnership [*koinōnia*] in the gospel from the first day until now" (1:5). Fellowship had taken concrete form in Christian giving.

Perhaps the classic passage concerning Christian fellowship is found in the prologue of 1 John:

> That which was from the beginning, which we have heard, which we have seen with our eyes, which we have looked upon and

touched with our hands, concerning the word of life—the life was made manifest, and we saw it, and testify to it, and proclaim to you the eternal life which was with the Father and was made manifest to us—that which we have seen and heard we proclaim also to you, so that you may have fellowship with us; and our fellowship is with the Father and with His Son Jesus Christ. And we are writing this that our joy may be complete (1:1-4).

Toward a Definition of Fellowship

Abuses of the word.—The word *fellowship*, like *love*, means different things to different people. Since fellowship is imperative in church life, we must find an acceptable definition of the word.

For many fellowship is the third word in announcements about parties and activities: food, fun, and fellowship. In that context, *fellowship* is getting together, being chummy, and enjoying each other's company. On that level everyone offers fellowship these days. Social activists, benevolent groups, service clubs, sewing circles, the corner tavern, and churches—all offer fellowship. It may be little more than coffee and doughnuts, punch and cookies, or ham and green beans at the church supper.

In reality that represents a corruption of the word *fellowship*. Christian fellowship must mean more than togetherness, feeling good, and feeling accepted. On that level the church would become little better than a social club, providing sharing and caring.

The meaning of the word.—Literally, the word *koinōnia* means sharing, having in common, or participation. It comes from a Greek verb meaning "to have a share in" or "to come into communion with." *Koinōnia* is God's gift to His children.

The church is a fellowship of loving concern. Christian fellowship is taking part in something with someone. Many modern-day churches tend to place more emphasis on "with someone" than on "in something." The result is that fellowship is considered nothing more than being together. However, the New Testament emphasis is on "in something." The early Christians were together for a purpose, whether the apostles' teaching, fellowship, breaking of bread, or the prayers (Acts 2:42).[7]

Illustrations of the word.—Paul's concept of the church as "the body of Christ" provides a good illustration of what is meant by the word *fellowship*. Each person in the church is not only a member of the body but also a member of all the other Christians who make up the body. They are so bound together that they feel keenly the hurts, sorrows, and joys that come to each other. That is *koinōnia*.

John provided another good illustration of fellowship when he described the disciples as branches in Jesus the vine (John 15:1-11). It is a vital union. "I am the vine," Jesus said, "you are the branches. He who abides in me, and I in him, he it is that bears much fruit, for apart from me you can do nothing" (v. 5). The branch is totally dependent on the vine for life and vitality. The branches are also dependent on each other for strength and productivity. That is *koinōnia*.

The Book of Acts contains a beautiful glimpse of the fellowship of the early church. On Paul's first missionary journey, stones were hurled at him outside Lystra, and he was left for dead: "As the disciples stood round about him, he rose up, and came into the city" (Acts 14:20, KJV). The world had done what it could to silence Paul. It left Paul for dead. Then the disciples came and formed a circle around him. They nursed his wounds. They gave him strength and encouragement. They put fresh heart and determination into him. Finally, on his own strength, he went back into the same city. The ministry of the church is to form a circle of love and concern around all believers in their times of need.[8] That is *koinōnia*.

In larger churches, Sunday School classes come nearest to being able to offer caring, personal ministry. When functioning at their best, they form circles of love and concern around their class members. They stay in contact with each other. They visit class members when they are sick or hospitalized. In times of dying or death, they bring food, run errands, attend memorial services, expressing sympathy. When a class member is hurting, they form a circle, offer encouragement, give strength, until that person is able to make it on his or her own again. That is *koinōnia*.

The Nature of Christian Fellowship

"Where two or three are gathered together in my name," Jesus said, "there am I in the midst of them" (Matt. 18:20, KJV). Jesus was not concerned with numbers in this passage. Rather, He was pointing to a vital principle of the Christian life—we are not meant to battle on our own. The Christian who avoids or neglects fellowship with other Christians may find the battle excessively tough, and he has only himself to blame. Fellowship is available. Christ has promised His presence.

A new dimension of togetherness.—Christian fellowship is different from other fellowships. In the early church, Jews and Gentiles, men and women shared the life and work of Christ. Slaves and free persons were joined together as equals. Race and nationality were transcended. Walls that divided people were broken down. All members were one in Christ. Membership depended solely upon one's relationship to Christ, the head of the body.

The fellowship of the church is unique. It has characteristics that are not found elsewhere. Most fellowship groups are exclusive. The gospel is for every person. Christian fellowship knows no boundaries of race, nation, class, age, or sex. In the church, we are all persons created in the image of God. Christian fellowship rises above class distinctions. The gospel is a great leveler. However, rather than leveling people *down* to a lower standard, it levels them *up* to a higher one.

Christian fellowship rises above race distinctions. God created all races. The church includes people of every race. All races are of equal worth in the sight of God. The task of the church is to create conditions conducive to the fullest development of all races.

The fellowship of the church transcends patriotism. It instills in Christ's followers a loyalty to God that is above loyalty to human beings. However, the result of such higher loyalty is that Chris-

tians become their nations' best citizens. But that is not all, they
recognize the church as a worldwide community that produces a
fellowship of understanding among all people.[9]

The Christian's highest privilege.—Most American Christians
take for granted their privilege of fellowship with other Christians. Christians in other parts of the world are not so fortunate.
"Behold, how good and pleasant it is when brothers dwell in
unity!" (Ps. 133:1). The physical presence of other Christians
should be a source of incomparable joy and strength for the believer. In fact, the Christian should yearn for such fellowship.

The potential blessings are inexhaustible for those privileged to
live in daily fellowship with other Christians. The one who has
that privilege should live in a constant state of gratitude to God.
"It is grace," said Bonhoeffer, "nothing but grace, that we are
allowed to live in community with Christian brethren."[10]

The Duties of Christian Fellowship

We are Christians not merely for our own sakes but for others.
Selfish Christianity is a contradiction of terms. After baptism the
Christian is included in a wider community. Changing times and
circumstances will alter our perception of the nature and mission
of that community.

Trends working against fellowship.—Quality fellowship is becoming increasingly difficult to achieve. Alvin Toffler in *Future
Shock* named transience, novelty, and diversity as the three primary change agents in today's world. These three trends not only
produce future shock but also play havoc with the fellowship level
of the church.

The trend toward transience in persons, places, and things
makes it difficult for churches to create community. This is the
day of the portable church, moving members, preferred anonym-
ity, casual commitment, and spasmodic training. A fellowship of
loving concern is a rare commodity.

The trend toward novelty in a superindustrialized society is also
making an impact on the church. This is the day of organ trans-

plants and genetic manipulation, fads and cults, deterioration of family and acceptance of singleness. The church's understanding of "family" is rapidly changing.

The trend toward diversity also affects the fellowship of the church. The individual faces many religious decisions. In the past the decision was simple. The choice was 1 of 8 to 10 major denominations. Now there are over 250 different denominations and cults. And the number is increasing daily. The problem is over choice. True fellowship is difficult to achieve.

E. Glenn Hinson identified growing individualism as an additional problem.[11] Each person insists on doing his or her own thing and deciding about his or her own beliefs. Some are predicting that the gathered congregation is a thing of the past.

What we owe each other.—Factors which make fellowship difficult also make it essential. The individual Christian needs the church. The church needs each Christian. The writer of Hebrews issued a challenge and a warning to every believer: "Let us consider how to stir up one another to love and good works, not neglecting to meet together, as is the habit of some but encouraging one another, and all the more as you see the Day drawing near" (10:24-25).

What is our duty to each other in the church? We have the responsibility of continuous care. We are to watch over one another, keep an eye on each other. In giving care, we are to stimulate each other to noble living. The fellowship of the church should provide a continuous incentive for brotherly love and right conduct.

We also owe it to each other to worship together regularly, "not neglecting to meet together, as is the habit of some." The writing of the New Testament was not complete when some believers formed the habit of not attending public worship.

A pastor told about one of his neighbors who had a beautiful boxer. One day the dog jumped the fence and roamed the neighborhood. The pastor watched as the frustrated dog tried to get a drink from a whirling sprinkler in his front yard. He was having some difficulty in synchronizing his head and tongue with the intermittent spurts of water. Christians experience a similar frustration. Many attempt to quench spiritual thirst through hit-and-miss church attendance. Instead of going to the fountain of still waters, they drop in occasionally for a "spurt of church."

Finally we owe each other mutual encouragement. One of the purposes of our public meetings is to offer mutual building up and encouragement. A church can well afford to lose almost anything before it can lose its fellowship of encouragement and loving concern.

Grady Nutt understood the nature of Christian fellowship. "I am who/what/whatever I am today," he said, "because of the Samaritans who have oiled my wounds and donkeyed me to help."[12]

Conclusion

When the church becomes a fellowship of loving concern, it will attract the attention of the outside world. Jesus said, "By this all men will know that you are my disciples, if you have love for one another" (John 13:35). The most persuasive of all qualities is that of genuine love and concern.

Would you like to become involved in a task that is of utmost importance to God? Then give your assistance in creating a fellowship of loving concern in your church.

Notes

1. IF THIS IS NOT A PLACE by Ken Medema © copyright 1977 by Word Music (A Div. of WORD, INC.) All rights reserved. International Copyright Secured. Used by permission.

2. James L. Sullivan, *Baptist Polity* (Nashville: Broadman Press, 1983), p. 21.

3. R. Newton Flew, *Jesus and His Church* (London: Epworth Press, 1938), pp. 97-98.

4. The outline for this section was suggested in an article by Dale Moody entitled, "The Nature of the Church," in *What Is the Church?*, edited by Duke McCall (Nashville: Broadman Press, 1958), pp. 15-27.

5. William Temple, *Readings in St. John's Gospel* (London: Macmillan & Co., Ltd., 1955), p. xvi.

6. Elton Trueblood, *The Incendiary Fellowship* (New York: Harper & Row, 1967), p. 108.

7. Ralph P. Martin, *The Family and the Fellowship* (Grand Rapids: Eerdmans, 1979), p. 36.

8. Lavonn D. Brown, *Truths that Make a Difference* (Nashville: Convention Press, 1980.), pp. 102-104.

9. Elmer G. Homrighausen, *I Believe in the Church* (Nashville: Abingdon Press, 1959), pp. 84-86.

10. Dietrich Bonhoeffer, *Life Together* (San Francisco: Harper & Row, 1954), p. 20.

11. E. Glenn Hinson, *The Integrity of the Church* (Nashville: Broadman, 1978), p. 21.

12. Grady Nutt, *So Good, So Far* (Nashville: Impact Books, 1979), p. 13.

2
The Priesthood of All Believers

The previous chapter defined the church as a fellowship of loving concern. To be a believer is to be a believer in fellowship. Members of the body are also members of one another. They are so bound together that they feel the hurts, sorrows, and joys that come to each other.

How individual members relate to each other is our next consideration. The priesthood of all believers is a biblical concept used to describe this relationship. All Christians have an equal right to direct access to God. The concept seems self-evident. Who would argue against it? Yet, few doctrines have been more misunderstood, misapplied, and inadequately expressed.

In the church each member must take upon himself the responsibility for the spiritual lives of the other members. Within the redemptive society, no single member should have to struggle alone in the battles of life. Trueblood called this our "unlimited liability." Jesus called it loving your neighbor as yourself (Matt. 19:19). Paul called it bearing one another's burdens (Gal. 6:2). Since the time of the Reformation, Baptists have been the chief exponents of the priesthood of all believers.

The concept of the priesthood of all believers does not mean that every Christian is an adequate priest unto himself, that church is unnecessary. It does mean that every Christian is a priest unto others, so Christian community is necessary.

The priesthood of all believers is a doctrine with two parts. The first part has to do with the believer's right of direct access to God without any human or institutional mediator. It insists that each Christian is capable of dealing directly with God.

The second part of the priesthood of all believers teaches that every Christian is a priest or minister and thus has a ministry to perform. While the first part is certainly true, we have failed to understand and adequately apply the second part. We have not always insisted that every believer has a spiritual responsibility to practice his priesthood in behalf of every other Christian. Trueblood described this failure:

> Most Protestants pay lip service to the Reformation doctrine of the priesthood of every believer, but they do not thereby mean to say that every Christian is a minister. Many hasten to add that all they mean by the familiar doctrine is that nobody needs to confess to a priest, since each can confess directly to God. The notion that this doctrine erases the distinction between laymen and minister is seldom presented seriously, and would, to some, be shocking, but it does not take much study of the New Testament to realize that the early Christians actually operated on this revolutionary basis.[1]

The church has been given a task too great for her. No professional clergy can do what the church is called to do. But the church has also been given a great weapon—a "priest at every elbow." What if the tame lay house cats should discover they really are "Christ, the Tiger"? What if the thousands of capable lay people came to understand the Christian life as a ministry to others? Our churches must come to an understanding of what God's design is for the laity.

All Christians who take the doctrine of the priesthood of all believers seriously and believe it applies to the twentieth century are obligated to seek out its meaning in the biblical materials.

The Teachings of the Old Testament

The priesthood of all believers, so clearly taught in the New Testament, has its roots in the Old Testament.

Beginning with Creation Itself

The idea of people's inherent capability of dealing with God for themselves goes back to creation. In the beginning human beings were created by God "in our image, after our likeness" (Gen. 1:26-27). In creation persons were given a spiritual nature akin to God. God is a person. He created human beings as persons. Therefore, mankind has the capacity for fellowship, communion, and responsiveness with the Creator.

Human beings were the crowning act of God's creation. God, as a person, could have fellowship only with another person. God is Spirit and human beings possess a spiritual nature. As infinite person, God can approach the finite person. And all people are capable of responding to God. Humanity's right of direct access to God was present from the beginning.

Reflected in the Abrahamic Covenant

God's covenant with Abraham was a grace covenant with no conditions attached. "And I will make of you a great nation," God said to Abraham, "and I will bless you, and make your name great, so that you will be a blessing . . . and by you all the families of the earth shall bless themselves" (Gen. 12:2-3).

So the right of direct access to God involves responsibility as well as privilege. The privilege is that "I will bless you." The responsibility is that "you will be a blessing."

Amplified in the Mosaic Covenant

The covenant God made with Moses at Sinai was a covenant of law and had conditions attached. God called a people to share His redemptive mission. The Lord said to Israel through Moses:

> You have seen what I did to the Egyptians, and how I bore you on eagles' wings and brought you to myself. Now therefore, if you will obey my voice and keep my covenant, you shall be my own possession among all peoples; for all the earth is mine, and you

shall be to me a kingdom of priests and a holy nation. These are the words which you shall speak to the children of Israel (Ex. 19:4-6).

This covenant was conditional. "If" you keep my covenant, "then" you shall be to me a kingdom of priests. Apparently, if Israel failed to fulfill the condition, God was no longer bound by the promise.

The Meaning of "a Kingdom of Priests"

Exodus 19:4-6 is the primary Old Testament text concerning Israel's priesthood. It must be understood in the larger context of Israel's relationship to God and her own self-understanding.

At the beginning of Hebrew history, no priestly class existed. In those early days, the head of the Hebrew household was the equivalent of a priest. He was not an official priest, but he had certain priestly duties.

Along the way, Israel became conscious of her special relationship as "the people of God." She came to be God's chosen people by revelation, by election, and by covenant. The new relationship came by divine initiative and not human merit.

When Israel became possessor of a written tradition and began to build temples, the need for an official priesthood emerged. At first priests were largely interpreters of the Word and the law and the will of God.

By the time of the post-Exilic period, the priesthood had undergone a complete change. The development of the sacrificial system, the hereditary nature of the priesthood, and the centralization of worship in Jerusalem resulted in greater power for the priest. He became the indispensable intermediary between men and God.

However, the Suffering Servant concept found in Isaiah provides the best transition to the New Testament doctrine of the priesthood of all believers. (See Isa. 42:1-4; 49:1-7; 50:4-9; 52:13 to 53:12.)

The covenant with Moses was conditional. As time progressed

it became increasingly evident that Israel would not keep her part of the agreement. She claimed the blessings and privileges but failed to carry out the mission and responsibilities. A new covenant was needed and promised:

> Behold, the days are coming, says the Lord, when I will make a new covenant with the house of Israel and the house of Judah, not like the covenant which I made with their fathers when I took them by the hand to bring them out of the land of Egypt, my covenant which they broke . . . says the Lord. But this is the covenant which I will make . . . I will put my law within them, and I will write it upon their hearts; and I will be their God, and they shall be my people (Jer. 31:31-33).

Under this new covenant each believer would be his own priest. Each would have direct access to God.

The Teachings of the New Testament

When Jesus came, the people were still living under the restrictions and subjugation of an official priesthood. They still believed that the only approach to God was through a priest. The Pharisees had emerged as the "separated ones" but had no sense of mission or ministry. Into that situation God sent His Son as the "one mediator between God and men, the man Christ Jesus" (1 Tim. 2:5).

The High Priesthood of Jesus

Jesus identified more readily with the Suffering Servant concept found in Isaiah (see 52:13 to 53:12) than with the idea of priesthood. When James and John requested places of power, Jesus responded, "For the Son of man also came not to be served but to serve, and to give his life as a ransom for many" (Mark 10:45). At the institution of the Lord's Supper, He said, "But I am among you as one who serves" (Luke 22:27).

A servant ministry identified.—Early in His ministry Jesus went to the synagogue in His hometown of Nazareth. On the sabbath day He attended worship "as his custom was." The attendant in-

vited Him to read and gave Him a scroll of the prophet Isaiah.
Jesus found the passage He wanted and stood to read:

> The Spirit of the Lord is upon me,
> because he has anointed me to preach the good news
>   to the poor.
> He has sent me to proclaim release to the captives
> and recovering of sight to the blind,
> to set at liberty those who are oppressed,
> to proclaim the acceptable year of the Lord.

Jesus rolled up the scroll, handed it to the attendant, and sat down.
The eyes of all those in the synagogue were still fixed on Him
when He said, "Today this scripture has been fulfilled in your
hearing" (Luke 4:16-21). Jesus would clearly be a Priest with
good tidings.

A gradual recognition of His high priesthood.—The high
priesthood of Jesus is implied in what is called Jesus' "High-
Priestly Prayer" in John 17. In this prayer Jesus offered Himself
for the sake of His disciples (v. 19) and interceded with the Father
in behalf of His disciples both present (vv. 9-17) and future
(vv. 20-23). These priestly functions were accepted quite readily
by Jesus.

If the high priesthood of Jesus is implied in John 17, it is specifically and carefully identified in the Epistle to the Hebrews. The
book has as its theme the superiority and all-sufficiency of Christ.
He is shown to be superior to the prophets, to angels, to Moses,
Joshua, and the Aaronic priesthood.

The unique obedience and deep devotion to God reflected in
Jesus' life and death made a deep impression on the Christian
community. So much so that the writer of Hebrews called Him
"the apostle and high priest of our confession" (3:1). It is impossible to conclude that the high priesthood of Jesus was simply a
continuation of the Old Testament priesthood. In fact, Christ was
revealed as having fulfilled and done away with the priesthood of

the Old Testament. That Christ's priesthood was superior to the
Aaronic priesthood was shown in Hebrews:

> Since then we have a great high priest who has passed through
> the heavens, Jesus, the Son of God, let us hold fast our confession.
> For we have not a high priest who is unable to sympathize with our
> weaknesses, but one who in every respect has been tempted as we
> are, yet without sin. Let us then with confidence draw near to the
> throne of grace, that we may receive mercy and find grace to help
> in time of need (4:14-16).

The Jewish high priest was "to offer gifts and sacrifices. . . .
for his own sins as well as for those of the people" (5:1,3). The
priests shared the sin problem which was a burden to the people.
They brought their own weakness to the sacrificial system. Jesus'
high priesthood was superior in that He was without sin (4:15).

The Jewish high priest offered both bloody and unbloody sacrifices of atonement for sins. These sacrifices were incomplete and
had to be repeated continually. Jesus' sacrifice was superior in that
He offered Himself a once-for-all effective sacrifice for sin.

> Therefore he is the mediator of a new covenant, so that those
> who are called may receive the promised eternal inheritance, since
> a death has occurred which redeems them from the transgressions
> under the first covenant. Nor was it to offer himself repeatedly, as
> the high priest enters the Holy Place yearly with blood not his own;
> for then he would have had to suffer repeatedly since the founda-
> tion of the world. But as it is, he has appeared once for all at the
> end of the age to put away sin by the sacrifice of himself.
>
> And every priest stands daily at his service, offering repeatedly
> the same sacrifices, which can never take away sins. But when
> Christ had offered for all time a single sacrifice for sins, he sat
> down at the right hand of God. (9:15,25-26; 10:11-12).

The Priesthood of All Christians

Even though one should believe in the high priesthood of Jesus,
does that necessarily lead to the concept of the priesthood of all
believers? Does the New Testament teach specifically and unam-

biguously that all Christians are priests? If so, where? The most direct references are found in 1 Peter and Revelation.

Christians called to be a royal priesthood.—Peter presented the primary text and actually borrowed terms from Exodus 19:4-6.

> Come to him, to that living stone, rejected by men but in God's sight chosen and precious; and like living stones be yourselves built into a spiritual house, to be a holy priesthood, to offer spiritual sacrifices acceptable to God through Jesus Christ.
>
> But you are a chosen race, a royal priesthood, a holy nation, God's own people, that you may declare the wonderful deeds of him who called you out of darkness into his marvelous light. Once you were no people but now you are God's people; once you had not received mercy but now you have received mercy (1 Pet. 2:4-5,9-10).

Perhaps Peter had in mind an imaginary opponent who said, "Access to God is available only to priests and only priests can offer sacrifices to God." Peter answered "That is true, but in Christ every believer is a priest." Peter challenged his Christian readers to be "built into a spiritual house, to be a holy priesthood, to offer spiritual sacrifices acceptable to God through Jesus Christ" (v. 5). All believers are priests and, therefore, can approach God directly.

Peter borrowed heavily from Exodus when he declared his readers to be "a chosen race, a royal priesthood, a holy nation, God's own people" (v. 9). Believers in Christ have been chosen for privilege, obedience, and service. They belong to a kingdom in which each citizen serves as a priest. They compose a nation that is different, set apart. They are a people belonging especially to God. Their worth is in His ownership.

Peter's choice of words underscore that Christians are members of a larger body. No Christian can live in isolation from his brethren. There must be no free-lance Christianity which acts as though the larger body does not exist.

The flip side of privilege is always responsibility. God has made

Christians His own people in order that "[we] may declare the wonderful deeds of him who called [us] out of darkness into his marvelous light [Christianity]" (v. 9). Christian responsibility lies in the areas of witness, evangelism, and mission.

Christians called to be a kingdom of priests.—The second primary source is found in Revelation. Revelation 1:6 refers to Christ who has "made us a kingdom, priests to his God and Father." Revelation also declares of the redeemed multitude from all nations that God "hast made them a kingdom/and priests to our God,/and they shall reign on earth" (5:10). Again, Revelation 20:6 predicts that Christians "shall be priests of God and of Christ."

Nowhere in the New Testament is the term *priest* used to refer to a charismatic gift (Rom. 12:4-8; 1 Cor. 12:4-11; 27-31; Eph. 4:7-14) or to a role of leadership (1 Tim. 3:1-13; 5:3-22; Titus 1:5-9) that belongs to certain Christians but not to all Christians. Priestly gifts and priestly functions are given to every believer. The argument establishing a special or clerical priesthood within Christianity must be based on something other than the New Testament.

Therefore, when one unites with the community of believers, when one accepts the priesthood of all believers, one is thereby uniting with Jesus in God's redemptive purpose in the world. This means that every believer must repent, confess, believe, and obey for oneself. No priest, sponsor, proxy, or authority is available. Are we ready to be priests unto ourselves and for each other?

The Teachings of History

The doctrine of the priesthood of all believers is clearly taught in both the Old and the New Testaments. Yet this doctrine continues to be threatened and challenged as it has been throughout history.

In the History of Judaism

Judaism's early history was characterized by no priestly class. The father in the home carried out priestly duties. The development of an official priesthood was gradual. Many influences made their contribution: a consciousness of being "the people of God," written tradition, building temples and synagogues, development of a sacrificial system, and the centralization of worship in Jerusalem. When Jesus came the religious life of the people had become a formal, legalistic, authoritarian system. The only approach to God was through the official priesthood.

In the History of Christianity

The cycle identified in Judaism repeated itself in the history of the Christian movement. In the coming of Christ a new movement was born. Quite early it became apparent that the new wine could not be contained in the old wineskins.

Relationship to God based on personal experience.—Jesus taught that it was necessary for people to be "born again" through their own personal faith in Him. He insisted that the essence of religion was in loving God supremely and loving one's neighbor as oneself. He offered abundant life to all who would follow. One could go directly to God in confession and find forgiveness. No priestly mediation was necessary.

For this Jesus was crucified. After Jesus' resurrection the movement continued to gain momentum in spite of obstacles and persecution. The church was a fellowship of these redeemed people. Its purpose was redemptive. It grew rapidly.

The movement toward institutionalism. At first church organization was simple and based primarily on need. During the first few centuries after Christ, the movement was toward centralized authority. Leading bishops began to emerge to preserve the purity of the faith against heresies and to administer the ordination of preachers and teachers.

By the fifth century or soon thereafter, the bishop of Rome gained supremacy over others; the Roman Catholic Church had begun. The change came about gradually. Relationship to God based on personal experience degenerated into an intellectual acceptance of dogma. Form and ceremony were substituted for personal experience.

Once again an official priesthood was developed. Direct access to God was not encouraged. One approached God through a priest or human mediator. The professional priesthood became the repository of the mysteries and grace of God. The common people were subjugated to the dominance of the priestly class. This led to oppression, hardship, and suffering. This was the plight of Christianity in the sixteenth century.

Leading to the Reformation

Early in the sixteenth century, rumblings were already being heard of a movement to recapture the inner spirit of religion. The movement would emphasize individual freedom and personal, experiential faith.

Martin Luther was the father of the Reformation movement. Three basic principles were at the heart of the Reformation: (1) justification by faith, (2) Scripture as the sole rule of faith and practice, and (3) the priesthood of all believers. Once again the movement was away from centralized authority and toward the importance of the individual. Luther said, "Every shoemaker can be a priest of God."

And on to the Present

A number of denominations have sought to uphold and apply the fundamental principles of the Reformation. Through the years, they have vigorously opposed infant baptism and insisted on the baptism of believer's only. These groups have been equally dedicated to religious freedom not only for themselves but for all people. They have insisted that all people should be able to worship God according to the dictates of their own consciences.

As one might expect, these same Christian groups have also been the chief exponents of the priesthood of every believer. They have sought earnestly to apply the doctrine of universal priesthood to every area of life. The heart of the gospel is found in Paul's Letter to the Ephesians:

> For by grace you have been saved through faith; and this is not your own doing, it is the gift of God—not because of works, lest any man should boast. For we are his workmanship, created in Christ Jesus for good works, which God prepared beforehand, that we should walk in them (2:8-10).

Contemporary Threats to the Doctrine

The movement that repeats itself in history is always away from individual freedom and toward centralized authority. Therefore, one might expect the doctrine of the priesthood of every believer to be continually threatened and challenged. It has been in every generation of believers.

Sometimes the doctrine of the priesthood of every believer is threatened openly, as in the development of a priestly class. Many Christians enjoy the comfort and security of a priestly class who will do their thinking, make their decisions, tell them what to believe about the Bible, and accept responsibility for them. History shows that a priestly class will make itself available to those Christians who are willing to surrender individual freedom.

At other times, the challenge to the doctrine of the priesthood of every believer is more subtle and indirect. It may be the simple insinuation that the believer is not capable of dealing directly with God for himself. The believer needs someone to "go to God" for him. It may be the simple suggestion that the Christian, especially in his early experience, needs a "spiritual leader" or a "spiritual authority" as a go-between to represent him to God. He needs someone responsible for him who will impose some system of checks and balances on his life.

Again, history shows that "spiritual authorities" are available in abundance for those Christians willing to relinquish their God-given privilege of direct access and approach to God.

The Privileges of Priesthood

What does the doctrine of the priesthood of every believer mean to the individual Christian? What are the privileges involved?

Direct Access to God

The most obvious privilege of priesthood is that of direct access and approach to God. In fact, many people never go beyond the idea that nobody needs to confess to a priest, since each can confess directly to God.

In Judaism only the high priest had access to the innermost part of the Temple, the holy of holies. He mediated there between God and the common people waiting outside. However, by His sacrificial death, Christ perfected and finished that kind of mediation and opened to all access to the holy of holies.

Christians no longer stand on the threshold of the Temple begging for grace through the priest as the holy middleman. They themselves stand in the very midst of the holy temple, as the priests chosen by God, able to communicate directly with God. This separates the believer from family, society, friendship, all sponsors, proxies, and human mediators. The priesthood of the believer places every Christian in an exclusive circle alone and face to face with God.

Direct Prayer to God

Closely related to direct access to God is the privilege of direct prayer to God. Part of what it means to be made "in the image of God" is that we are persons as He is a person. This means we have the capacity for communion with, responsiveness to, and fellowship with God. Prayer is the highest form of communion.

This possibility of close relationship with God is often forfeited under the priestly system. Since the priest is considered a mediator between God and man, believers often assume that they must go through the priest in order to reach God. The worshipers are once removed from direct prayer to God.

The doctrine of the priesthood of every believer restores the privilege of praying directly to God through Jesus Christ. The confession of sin directly to God is the privilege of every Christian.

The Right of Interpretation of Scripture

Another privilege of priesthood is the right to read and interpret Scripture for oneself under the leadership of the Holy Spirit. At times in history, the Bible has been confined to the place of worship and available only to the priestly class. The official priesthood emerged as the only competent interpreters and teachers of the Word and the Law. Laypeople were actually discouraged in their attempts to read and understand the Bible for themselves.

The Reformation and the revival of the doctrine of the priesthood of all believers changed all that. Every Christian, as a priest, is given the charge to learn and to teach. The responsibility of intellectual inquiry into the meaning of the Scriptures rests squarely with every Christian. With respect to the interpretation of Scripture, each believer-priest has the right to do as he is led by the Holy Spirit.

The competency of the soul in religion has been a precious article of faith among many Christians. At the same time, it is constantly threatened and challenged. When one person or group of persons tries to coerce others to interpret the Bible exactly as they do, the priesthood of believers is violated.

The Responsibilities of Priesthood

The Offering of "Spiritual Sacrifices"

The principal function of Christians as priests is "to offer spiritual sacrifices acceptable to God through Jesus Christ" (1 Pet. 2:5). These are spiritual sacrifices in contrast to the material sacrifices of Old Testament priests. For the Christians, any act or service in the kingdom of God is a priestly act.

A spiritual sacrifice of worship.—The Epistle to the Hebrews declares: "Through him [Christ] then let us continually offer up a sacrifice of praise to God, that is, the fruit of lips that acknowledge his name" (13:15). The priestly function of believers is evident in Paul's exhortation to Christians to present themselves "a living sacrifice, holy and acceptable to God, which is your spiritual worship" (Rom. 12:1). Every Christian must make this sacrifice. We take our cue from Jesus, the great High Priest, who willingly offered Himself as a sacrifice for us.

A spiritual sacrifice of witness.—Those who are the "royal priesthood" are to "declare the wonderful deeds of him who called you out of darkness into his marvelous light" (1 Pet. 2:9). Evangelism and missions may be considered extensions of the priestly functions of believers.

A spiritual sacrifice of stewardship.—One expression of mutual concern is mutual giving. Gifts given by the Philippian Christians for Paul in his proclamation of the gospel to the Gentiles were "a fragrant offering, a sacrifice acceptable and pleasing to God" (4:18). The practice of faithful stewardship is a part of the Christian's function as a priest.

A spiritual sacrifice of service.—The author of the Epistle to the Hebrews admonished his readers: "Do not neglect to do good and to share what you have, for such sacrifices are pleasing to God" (13:16). The sacrifices of Christians as priests are also to be in the nature of ministering service.

Everything the Christian does is done for God. Singing, praying, giving, worshiping, sharing faith, holy living, and acts of service are all activities of the kingdom of priests which God has made of Christians.

Becoming Priests Unto Others

Believers also have a priestly function in relation to others. The Latin word for priest is *pontifex* which means bridge-builder. Christian priests must build some bridges that help bring other people to God and God to people. Therefore, each believer must accept responsibility for the spiritual lives of other believers.

Every Christian must practice a spiritual priesthood in behalf of fellow Christians. Christian priests are to make intercession for all people: "First of all, then, I urge that supplications, prayers, intercessions, and thanksgivings be made for all men" (1 Tim. 2:1). We are to go to God for others.

As Christians we must live near enough to God to make Him real to other people. We must be good listeners, allow others to confess, and assist them in seeking and finding God's forgiveness.

The Implications of Priesthood

The priesthood of the believer means that the church with an active minister and a passive supporting laity can no longer serve as our model.

The Call Is for All

There is a difference between God's basic call to ministry which is issued to all Christians and His call for special or professional ministry. But all believers are called to minister.

The New Testament contains evidence of an "official ministry." Some are called for certain specialized ministries like apostles, prophets, evangelists, pastors and teachers (Eph. 4:11). Paul described their work as being "for the perfecting of the saints, for the work of the ministry, for the edifying of the body of Christ" (v. 12, KJV). However, the comma after "saints" is not in the Greek text. The primary task of the official ministry, then, is to equip the saints for the work of the ministry.

All Christians are called to minister. Just as certain people go to seminary because they have been called by God to professional ministry, every Christian should unite with a church because he or she has been called by God to Christian ministry. The church is responsible for equipping believers for their ministry.

The current distinction between the clergy and the laity, the sacred and the secular, the professional ministry and the "ordinary" Christian was not so clearly defined in the New Testament. The early Christian fellowship made no distinction between part time and full time, totally committed and partially committed. In the royal priesthood, all Christians are called to the ministry.

The Church's Greatest Untapped Resource

Many laypeople have found comfort in the idea of an "official ministry" paid to do God's work. It is not unusual to hear such statements as, "That's his job. We hired him to do it. If he can't do it, let's get someone who can." In many churches today, the laity seems to have the attitude that the primary responsibility for ministry rests in the hands of the clergy.

No wonder the task of the church remains too great for her. The professional clergy will never be able to do what the church is called to do. The laity, the new people of God, is the greatest unused resource available to the church. Our churches must recapture the ministry of the laity. What if thousands of capable laypeople began to understand their calling to minister to others? What if hundreds of capable ministers began to accept their calling to equip the saints for the work of the ministry?

How does the priesthood of the believer work? Each and every believer is a priest wherever that person is. That means that there is a priest at every elbow.

Our Ministry in the World

Could it be that we still rely on the wrong people for our ministry in the world? The minister, called to professional service, centers his ministry in the church—the gathered community. Even though he is involved in the lives of his people in other places, most of his efforts are directed toward planning and preparing for those specified times when the church is gathered in order to equip Christ's followers for their ministry.

On the other hand, the primary ministry of the laity must be performed in the world—the scattered community. The gathered church must create a strong centrifugal force which thrusts Christian priests back out into the world. The testimony concerning the early church was that "those who were scattered went about preaching the word" (Acts 8:4).

The Christian life is characterized by a rhythm of come and go. Christ's commands to His followers reveal a creative tension between invitation and commission. On the one hand, He invited, "Come to me . . . and I will give you rest" (Matt. 11:28). On the other hand, He urged, "Go therefore and make disciples of all nations" (Matt. 28:19).

That come-and-go rhythm continues to characterize the tension in the lives of Christians. There are times when we should assemble—come together; there are times when we should be scattered—go out. The priesthood of the believer means that the primary ministry of the Christian laity is *in the world*.

Therefore, on Monday the church is where you are as a Christian layperson: on the job, at home with your family, in your leisure hours, in the shop, in the office, on the farm, in the health club, or at the social gathering. The minister as clergy can be at only one place. Laypeople must become the ministers of the church in the world during the week. This is where most of their time is spent. Ministry to the world is yours. It's not that you ought to pitch in and help out; it is that you are the only hope for a priest at every elbow.

What is the primary aim of the church then? Is it to enlist and train laypeople for its organizations and services? Or is it to put theologically capable laypeople out in the world for service?

What is the primary aim of the Christian minister? Is it to plan worship, witness to the lost, and keep the organizational life of the church running smoothly? Or is it to equip the Christian priests for their ministry in the world?

What is the primary aim of the Christian layperson? Is it to attend church meetings, serve on committees, and see to the church's survival? Or is it to be priests to each other and priests in the world?

The key word here is *primary*. As Jesus instructed, "These you ought to have done, without neglecting the others" (Matt. 23:23). The greatest need of today's church is a new emergence of strong, capable laypeople. If the priesthood of the believer is true, then, only as the laypeople are strong, can our churches be strong. Whoever, wherever we are, whatever we do, we are ministers of God.[2]

Notes

1. Elton Trueblood, *Your Other Vocation* (New York: Harper & Bros., 1952), p. 30.

2. For further study the reader will find the following especially helpful: see Findley B. Edge, *A Quest for Vitality in Religion.* (Nashville: Broadman, 1963), especially the chapter entitled "The Priesthood of Believers and the Christian Life," p. 94 *f.* See Carlyle Marney, *Priests to Each Other* (Valley Forge: Judson Press, 1974). See *New Testament Studies,* edited by Huber Drumright and Curtis Vaughn, (Waco: Baylor University Press, 1975), the essay by James Leo Garrett, Jr., entitled "The Biblical Doctrine of the Priesthood of the People of God," p. 137 *f.*

3

Discipleship and Discipline

The Bible presents salvation in three tenses: past, present, and future. Most discussions about salvation are related to the past. "So, I have become a Christian," George began. "I filled out the card. I was baptized. I joined your church. Now what?" It's a good question. What happens after the past experience?

Some Christians become absorbed in speculation about the future. They become enamored with the signs of the times, evidence of the second coming of Christ, and prophecy concerning the future. In some cases, this overshadows their interest in salvation in the present tense.

This chapter considers salvation as a present, continuing process. The Christian life is the development of a Christlike personality. One is not born full grown physically. Neither is one reborn full grown spiritually. The maturing process takes a lifetime.

Definitions

Writers use many different words trying to express the new life that flows from union with Christ. The words *disciple, discipleship,* and *discipline* all come from the same Greek rootage. All three are essential to our understanding of Christian life.

Disciples

Jesus called people as followers. These followers became known as Jesus' disciples. The noun *disciple* comes from the verb meaning "to learn." It implies personal participation. The disciple is a learner, sitting at the feet of Christ. The self-image of the early church was that of a company of disciples who would learn from Christ (Eph. 4:20-21; Heb. 5:8-9). The supreme ambition of the disciple is simply to be like one's teacher.

Discipleship

Discipleship refers to the quality of life the disciple is expected to live. Discipleship involves a radical decision to be with Jesus. We live with the fallacy that church membership equals Christian discipleship. Obviously, that is not true. Authentic discipleship involves a careful and lifelong obedience to Christ's commands.

Discipline

Discipline refers to the instruction or training given to the disciple. In its positive form, *discipline* refers to a process of teaching and training (discipleship). In its negative form, it refers to corrective or reformative measures. The disciple must submit to the discipleship and discipline of the Christian life as the necessary parts of the total salvation experience.

Discipleship: A Process of Growth

The chasm between church membership and Christian discipleship has been a long-standing problem. A part of that problem is over-familiarity. *Disciples, discipleship,* and *discipline* are words we have heard many times. The result is that the committed Christianity of the New Testament has become a vague religiosity. The believer, injected with a mild form of Christianity, has been immunized against the real thing.

It is not uncommon to hear reasonings like this, "Religion is a private and personal matter. It's nobody else's business. It's just between God and me. I don't like church. I don't like worship." Why? Because genuine church membership (discipleship) involves heavy responsibilities of living in a way that pleases Jesus. Such concepts are a caricature of the religion of Jesus Christ. For many, discipleship has become giving to the Community Chest, maintaining an uncostly church membership, and having some degree of fidelity to marriage vows.

The New Testament Emphasis on Growth

The idea that growth is both needed and expected is one of the New Testament's central themes. The rate of growth varies from Christian to Christian. But the need is universal.

Christ's Great Commission implies the need for development in the Christian life: "Go therefore and make disciples of all nations, baptizing them . . . teaching them to observe all that I have commanded you" (Matt. 28:19-20). The implication is that new Christians are undeveloped and need to be taught how to live as Christians. Regeneration is a new birth; discipleship is a process of growth.

Jesus set forth the spiritual life and the kingdom of God in terms of living, growing things. He compared the kingdom to seed sown in different types of soil. The growth pattern of the seed was dependent on the quality of the soil (see Mark 4:1-20). He compared kingdom growth to the varying stages in the growing seed. "The earth produces of itself, first the blade, then the ear, then the full grain in the ear" (v. 28). Jesus' parable of the mustard seed showed His own faith in the ultimate growth of the kingdom: "It [the kingdom] is like a grain of mustard seed, which, when sown upon the ground, is the smallest of all the seeds on earth; yet when it is sown it grows up and becomes the greatest of all shrubs, and puts forth large branches, so that the birds of the air can make nests in its shade" (vv. 31-32).

Paul clearly expressed the progressive nature of salvation when he wrote, "The word of the cross is folly to those who are perishing, but to us who are being saved it is the power of God" (1 Cor. 1:18). In all of Paul's preaching and teaching, he had the goal in mind "that we may present every man mature in Christ" (Col. 1:28). Maturity is not automatic or instantaneous; it is gradual and by deliberate intent.

Paul expressed disappointment when Christians failed to show progress and development. He rebuked the Corinthians because they were still carnal and babes in Christ: "But I, brethren, could not address you as spiritual men, but as men of the flesh, as babes in Christ. I fed you with milk, not solid food; for you were not ready for it; and even yet you are not ready, for you are still of the flesh" (1 Cor. 3:1-3). Being a babe in Christ is not wrong unless that babyhood becomes unduly prolonged.

That which is living is expected to grow. Lack of growth should cause distress and alarm. The author of Hebrews reproved his readers because he could not see evidence of the growth he felt he had a right to expect:

For though by this time you ought to be teachers, you need some-one to teach you again the first principles [ABC's] of God's word. You need milk, not solid food; for every one who lives on milk is unskilled in the word of righteousness, for he is a child. But solid food is for the mature. . . . Therefore, let us leave the elementary doctrines of Christ and go on to maturity (Heb. 5:12 to 6:1).

A sad but true fact is that many Christians who by now should be demonstrating evidences of maturity are still enjoying playpens and sandboxes. All these Scripture passages point to the same conclusion. The New Testament teaches that "it's OK to grow."[1]

Growth Begins in Christian Conversion

The only imperative in the Great Commission is to "make disciples." Evidently Jesus intended the church to direct its active energies toward the making of disciples. The church is a company of disciples.

Few advantages can compare with being well-born. A Christian is a Christ-one. The past experience of repentance and faith has brought the believer into right relationship with God. The commitment to follow Christ is intended to be lifelong and life-changing. Baptism is an outward sign of the Christian's willingness to take on the life of discipleship. Now what?

Evangelism is a primary task of the church. Salvation is the beginning, but only the beginning, of the Christian life. A lifetime of growth is ahead. Our temptation, after leading someone to faith in Christ, is to sing, " 'Tis done—the great transaction's done." In reality it has only begun.

A wise observer in a fast-growing church said, "We have reached a lot of new people. It's exciting. I'm grateful. But we are doing a poor job of 'teaching them to observe all things.' They do not understand our beliefs. They do not accept responsibility. We lose them out the back door as fast as we bring them in the front." What can be done?

Growth Continues in a Life of Learning

From the beginning, the church has been a fellowship of learning. Commitment is a necessary beginning but is far from being the end. At conversion believers enter upon new life and set their faces in a fresh direction. "Therefore, if any one is in Christ," Paul wrote, "he is a new creation; the old has passed away, behold, the new has come" (2 Cor. 5:17).

Growth and the Christian.—The Christian life holds many options. Growth is not one of them. Because we have urged developing in the Christian life, apparently many feel they have an option. Evidently they choose not to grow.

Have you noticed what happens when a branch is successfully grafted into the trunk of a tree? The branch and the trunk enter into a vital relationship; life begins to flow from the trunk to the branch. Growth is evidence that a vital union has taken place. Failure to grow is evidence that a vital union has not taken place.

One freely chooses whether one will be a Christian. But, once the decision to be one of Christ's followers has been made, the nature of the new relationship involves growth. For the church to have to beg and plead for its members to grow, to train for service, or to fulfill their ministry is inconsistent with the essential nature of the Christian life.

Growth and sufficient time.—The process of growth toward maturity *is* the Christian life. This process will take time—

perhaps a long time. One Christian may require more time than another. I could have been spared much anguish and disappointment if someone had told me that in my early years as a Christian. I had no idea how long it took to mature spiritually. All I remember is that I was seldom satisfied with my rate of growth.

I am told that a guinea pig can care for itself within three days after birth. A human being will spend nearly a fourth of life growing up physically. In our physical, mental, and emotional growth, we experience *certain well-defined stages:* infancy, childhood, adolescence, young adulthood, and mature adulthood.

We experience a similar growth pattern in our spiritual development. During our spiritual infancy and childhood, we are largely dependent on others to supply our needs. Our childhood faith is mostly inherited. We believe because we are a part of a believing community. Given a proper atmosphere for growth, our faith should take on a more personal quality during late childhood or early adolescence. Personal commitment to Christ and baptism may be the result. The desire to belong to something bigger than we are (the church) is strong during these years.

During late adolescence and early adulthood, believers frequently experience a crisis of faith. The faith which has been more emotional is now putting down intellectual roots. For many this is a time of questioning, searching, and even criticism. This searching faith may act against earlier experiences. However, if good questions receive good answers, there is no reason why struggling faith should not become an owned or possessed faith. At this point the Christian should achieve a good balance of head and heart. The result will be a mature, adult faith adequate for adult years. Paul described this process: "When I was a child, I spoke like a child, I thought like a child, I reasoned like a child; when I became a man, I gave up childish ways" (1 Cor. 13:11).

Growing up spiritually *takes time, patience, and discipline.* The rate of progress may vary from person to person. Some will grow to Christian maturity more rapidly than others. Others will grow more like a tree grows—slowly, almost imperceptibly.

Yet we are all in the process of becoming what God wants us to be. We can be thankful that God does not expect us to be mature saints overnight. On the other hand, He does expect us to keep moving in that direction.

My big problem was determining the rate of growth that was right for me. I found myself pulled from all sides by the advice and criticism from zealous peers and well-meaning leaders. I remember the sense of relief when I realized that we are each unique in nature. God deals with each of His children differently. No one pattern fits all.

The difficulty is in *discovering a good balance* in Christian growth. Often the new believer will bounce back and forth between two extremes. On one hand, some believers mature too slowly. Perhaps they have never grasped the idea that growth is not optional. They neglect spiritual disciplines. They get locked in at some early stage of development or regress to some more comfortable stage. In any case the result is discouragement, disappointment, and growth failure. This problem was already present in the church by the time the New Testament was written (see 1 Cor. 3:1-3; Heb. 5:12 to 6:1).

On the other hand, some believers mature too rapidly for their own good. Their goal is to achieve spiritual maturity overnight. Since this is not possible, they often assume a spiritual maturity they do not possess. They feel they can bypass the normal stages of growth that others must go through. The person who, in his own mind, has discovered a shortcut to maturity is often quite obnoxious. The result is spiritual pride.

The church is often to blame. We have failed to heed the biblical warning, "Lay hands suddenly on no man" (1 Tim. 5:22, KJV). We take spiritual babes and project them into places of prominence long before they are ready. We take people from non-Christian backgrounds and make them overnight sensations on the evangelical testimony circuit. We expect spiritual babes to do the work of the mature. Often the result is embarrassment both to the new convert and the church.

The way of wisdom includes balance and good timing. Each Christian must discover his or her own pace or rate of growth. If it is different from others, so what? Perhaps that person marches to a different drummer. Few spiritual prodigies become mature Christians overnight.

No shortcuts to maturity are available. We live in a day when we can have almost anything instantly: coffee, tea, soup, cakes, milk, dinners—even mashed potatoes. We would like some kind of mix to which we add water, heat, stir, and "poof"—instant spiritual maturity. But it doesn't happen that way. Instant Christian maturity is not a marketable item.

Someone has observed that when God wants to make an oak, He takes a hundred years. When He wants to make a squash, He takes six weeks. The meteor which flashes across the sky leaving a brilliant trail of light draws a lot of attention and is burned out in the process. The star shining brightly year after year draws little attention, but navigators set their courses by it.

The one area where God never seems to be in a hurry is in the development of mature Christians. The followers of Christ need to realize that the pressure is off. The Christian life is intended to be a slow but steady growth toward maturity. We grow little by little, over a period of time—days, weeks, months, years. Jesus said, "Consider the lilies of the field, how they grow" (Matt. 6:28). How do lilies grow? They simply give expression to the life of God within. And how do we grow? By simply allowing God to express His life through us. We can't live all of life at the excitement point.

Growth and certain disciplines.—To suggest that growth in the Christian life is not optional does not mean to imply that it is automatic. No magic formula has been discovered which ensures Christian growth. The Bible, however, does call us to certain disciplines that contribute directly to our advancement in the Christian life. These are internal disciplines we must impose upon ourselves.

In order to grow as Christians, we must *put off some things while putting on others*. Christians are expected to leave behind some habits and practices of pre-Christian living. These things are judged as detrimental to the purpose of our new mission. Paul listed some of these things:

> Put to death therefore what is earthly in you: [immorality], impurity, passion, evil desire, and covetousness, which is idolatry. In these you once walked, when you lived in them. But now put them all away: anger, wrath, malice, slander, and foul talk from your mouth. Do not lie to one another, seeing that you have put off the old nature with its practices and have put on the new nature, which is being renewed in knowledge after the image of its creator (Col. 3:5,7-10).

Christians are expected, on the other hand, to put on some habits and practices that suit God's chosen people. These new practices are to be put on because they are necessary to accomplishing the purpose of the Christian mission. Paul also mentioned some of these things:

> Put on then, as God's chosen ones, holy and beloved, compassion, kindness, lowliness, meekness, and patience, forbearing one another and, if any has a complaint against another, forgiving each other; as the Lord has forgiven you, so you almost must forgive. And above all these [like an outer garment] put on love, which binds everything together in perfect harmony. And let the peace of Christ rule in your hearts. . . . And be thankful, Let the word of Christ dwell in you richly, as you teach and admonish one another in all wisdom (Col. 3:12-16).

A Christianity that does not change a person is imperfect. Ideally it begins immediately to recreate new Christians into what they are meant to be.

The growth process requires proper nourishment and *the regular practice of certain disciplines*. Believers must develop strong, good habits which will expel the weak, evil habits in their lives.

Christians are expected to live disciplined lives. For that reason, believers must take seriously some habits of obedience. A minimum list of these disciplines should include corporate worship, daily prayer, Bible reading and study, stewardship of talents and money, service, witness, and fellowship with other believers.

We envy the spiritually mature. We long to be where they are in the process. We forget that their journey took time and dedication. They got where they are one step at a time. It is the same for us. Jesus didn't say, "Come to me and get it over with." Rather, He said: "If any man would come after me, let him deny himself and take up his cross daily and follow me" (Luke 9:23). *Daily* is the key word.

In the Christian life there is always room for growth. It is like mountain climbing. We reach the top of one peak only to discover the summit is still before us. Complete maturity is never achieved in this life. Yet, we must keep the goal before our eyes.[2]

Growth Results in a Mature Faith

Given adequate time, a favorable atmosphere, and the regular practice of spiritual disciplines, the result should be a faith adequate for adult needs. Mature faith will be the unique possession of the individual Christian. It may not be exactly like someone else's, but it will be adequate for the one who possesses it. "So that we may no longer be children," Paul wrote, "tossed to and fro and carried about with every wind of doctrine, . . . Rather, speaking the truth in love, we are to grow up in every way into him who is the head, into Christ" (Eph. 4:14-15).

Discipleship is the positive side of church discipline, the side that refers to a process of teaching and training. In this sense, discipleship is the quality of life the disciple is expected to live. "Thus," wrote Findley Edge, "formative church discipline is that process of teaching and training by which the Christian is increasingly formed in the image of Christ."[3] There is another side of church discipline. It is not so popular. Nor has much been written about it.

Discipline: A Process of Reclamation

The word *discipline* is unpopular in our time. It evokes numerous negative mental images. Generally, we think only of exclusion from the church when we think of discipline. We have all heard tales of people who were "kicked out of the church" in days gone by. During the eighteenth century, John Wesley was noted for his habit of purging Methodist societies of nominal members. On one occasion he boasted of having reduced one society from eight hundred to four hundred members and insisted that the half was more than the whole!

The church has overreacted to such extremes. In an effort to miss the ditch on one side of the road, she has fallen in the ditch on the other side. Except in isolated cases, the church in the twentieth century makes no effort at corrective or reformative discipline. Little is said or written on the subject. Is a balance of freedom and responsibility possible? Is it too much to insist that the disciple submit to the discipline of the Christian life? Do we go too far when we insist that without discipline there can be no discipleship?

The Practice of Christian Discipline in the New Testament

Reformative or corrective discipline consists of the efforts of the church to deal with "occasions of scandal" within the fellowship. The church has three primary concerns: (1) the purity of doctrine, (2) the exemplary lives of members, and (3) the unity of fellowship. Therefore the church has every reason to be concerned when there is evidence of corrupt teaching (heresy), immoral behavior (sin), or a threat to fellowship (schism).

The early New Testament church did practice Christian discipline. Each individual case was handled on its own merits. Today one occasion may call for self-discipline (Matt. 5:23-24); another occasion may require congregational discipline (1 Cor. 5:1-13). At one time private discipline may be more appropriate; as a last resort it may be necessary to "tell it to the church." Some offenders may be dealt with gently and reclaimed without extreme measures (2 Cor. 2:5-11). Blatant offenders may need to be excommunicated first and reclaimed later (1 Cor. 5:1-13). Apparently, no one pattern for Christian discipline fits every occasion. Wisdom and patience are required. Let's look more carefully at some primary examples of New Testament discipline.

An example given by Jesus.—The passage most often cited gives advice on what to do in the case of differences between Christians. In Matthew 18:15-18, Jesus gave the procedure the Christian is to follow in seeking reconciliation with a brother who has wronged him:

> If your brother sins against you, go and tell him his fault, between you and him alone. If he listens to you, you have gained your brother. But if he does not listen, take one or two others along with you, that every word may be confirmed by the evidence of two or three witnesses. If he refuses to listen to them, tell it to the church; and if he refuses to listen even to the church, let him be to you as a Gentile and a tax collector.

Jesus encouraged private discipline and reclamation. Imagine how the peace of the church would be disturbed if every private difference and disagreement of members were paraded before her. Only as a last resort should it be reported to the church.

Jesus also told the parable concerning the tares (weeds) sown among wheat (see Matt. 13:24-30,36,43). The weeds closely resembled the wheat. Zealous workers urged the householder, "Then do you want us to go and gather them?" (v. 28). "But he said, 'No; lest in gathering the weeds you root up the wheat along with them. Let both grow together until the harvest'" (vv. 29-30). The wise householder knew it was impossible to pluck up the weeds without destroying good wheat in the process. Sometimes it is not easy to distinguish the good from the bad. God is the better judge. Some things are best left until judgment.

An example given by Paul.—In another well-known passage, Paul described how the church must deal with blatant offenders who have grievously sinned and dishonored the purity of the church:

> It is actually reported that there is immorality among you, and of a kind that is not found even among pagans; for a man is living with his father's wife. And you are arrogant! Ought you not rather to mourn? Let him who has done this be removed from among you. . . . I have already pronounced judgment in the name of the Lord Jesus on the man who has done such a thing. . . . you are to deliver this man to Satan for the destruction of the flesh, that his spirit may be saved in the day of the Lord Jesus (1 Cor. 5:1-5).

Apparently a man was living in an illicit relationship with his own step-mother. The church's attitude had been closely akin to pagan indifference. Paul's verdict was that the man had to be dealt with. He was to be delivered over to Satan's domain—the world where Satan holds sway.

In this case, Paul gave the incestuous person no opportunity to repent, confess, or seek forgiveness. Valid evidence of sincere repentance requires time. To come to true repentance takes time. The church had no time to wait; therefore, the exclusion of the wrongdoer was instant. Obviously, the church would try to help the offender *after* excommunication, *not before*.

Such discipline is never exercised for the satisfaction of the person who exercises it, but always for the mending of the person who has sinned, and always for the sake of the church. The action is always remedial, "that his spirit may be saved" (v. 5). It is also for the purity of the church (see 1 Cor. 5:6-13). Discipline must never be vengeful; it must always be curative. The goal is reclamation. Such discipline requires wisdom and patience.

On other occasions New Testament writers discussed how to deal with unsound teachings and threats to the fellowship (1 Tim. 6:3,5; 2 Tim. 2:16-19; Titus 3:10-11; and 2 John 9-11).

Alternatives Available to the Church

In the light of clear New Testament teachings, what is the

twentieth-century church to do? What are the alternatives to be considered?

A return to some form of church discipline.—Many voices are calling for a return to some form of Christian discipline. Such people are aware that corrective discipline was practiced by the early New Testament church. They know that the principle of discipline remains a valid teaching of the New Testament. Therefore, they feel that discipline should be taken seriously by any church genetically connected to the New Testament.

These people might even agree with the profound reasons why reformative discipline was easier and more practical in the first century. The churches were small. In many instances they were house churches. Each member was known intimately. They were like one big family. Discipline within the church membership was not unlike what one might expect within any family group.

In the first century, the contrast between the Christian walk and the pagan life-style was dramatically distinct. In fact, many of the church members were converted pagans. The teachings of Christ were, in many respects, a direct reversal of their former practices. Many practices considered evil by Christian standards were commonly accepted as normal behavior in the pagan world. Where lines of demarcation were so clearly drawn, church discipline would be easier.

Even though churches today differ in size from early churches, some believers insist that the disciple must submit to the discipline of the Christian life. The truth remains that without discipline there can be no discipleship.

Reformative discipline "virtually impossible" today.—Some believers today insist that corrective discipline is no longer a viable option for the church. They view it as a puritanical appendage of early church life. They consider any form of discipline as unthinkable in this enlightened age of tolerance. The reasons for no longer practicing church discipline are numerous.

For one thing, the difference between the Christian and non-Christian life-style is no longer so dramatic. Today, Christian principles have so permeated society that many people who make absolutely no claim to being Christian nevertheless live good moral lives. Also sin is so prevalent in the lives of church members that church discipline would be difficult to implement. Where would one begin, and who would initiate it?

Churches have grown larger and larger. People are casually admitted to membership. Churches have become so geared to numerical increase that biblical knowledge, theological competence, and ethical sensitivity are ignored. Add to this the two thousand years of influence from backslidden Christians and those who live undisciplined lives.

Reaction against the flagrant misuse and abuse of church discipline in the past also must be considered. We have heard the accounts of erroneous, unjust, and unchristian practices of church discipline. Churches in the late nineteenth and early twentieth centuries went too far. Church members were censured and excluded from fellowship for comparatively trivial faults. Church discipline fell into disfavor because the purpose became more vengeful and less remedial.

Many people consider that the practice of church discipline today would be a major disruptive force in the life of the church. After all, leading members and influential people might be involved. The peace of the church would be threatened. To begin making judgments now could become confusing. It would be seen as critical, not corrective; ruinous, not redemptive. It would be impossible to pluck up the weeds without destroying good wheat in the process.

Suggestions concerning church discipline.—Both of the preceding alternatives have strong arguments in their favor. What does it mean to be "the people of God" in today's world? What are we to do about church discipline? Those questions need further study both in general principles, and in particular cases as they arise in church life. However, the following suggestions may be helpful.

1. The church must *give more attention to formative, developmental discipline*. Preventive dentistry is more effective and less

painful than corrective dentistry. So is preventive discipline. The church may need to take another look at membership policies and the quality of instruction given new converts. The church educational program must accept responsibility for nurturing members in sound doctrine, sound Christian character, and sound unity. Everything the church does in Bible study, training, worship, and fellowship is a part of the process of formative, developmental discipline.

2. Any program of reformative discipline must *seek a balance of freedom and responsibility*. While the church continues to hold up the ideal, it must continue also to be loving, forgiving, accepting, and redemptive. A sense of timing is crucial. Any corrective discipline must be prompt, kind, and wise. The more seldom one rebukes, the more effective the rebuke is.

Jesus reflected a good sense of timing in dealing with the woman taken in adultery (John 8:1-11). The Pharisees and scribes said, "Now in the law Moses commanded us to stone such" (v. 5). The strict, letter-of-the-law approach was clear. Jesus said, "Neither do I condemn you; go, and do not sin again" (v. 11). He would not add the weight of His personal condemnation to the weight she already bore. Wisdom is in knowing when and when not to apply the letter of the law.

3. Any form of corrective *discipline should be handled privately*. As much as possible, it must be kept between the offender and the one authorized to bring discipline. Jesus encouraged private discipline and reclamation. The larger our churches become, the more impractical it becomes to "tell it to the church." Only when all else fails should it be reported to the church, if at all.

4. *The biblical purpose of discipline must be retained*. Reformative discipline must be redemptive, not punitive; corrective, not critical. Discipline must always be grounded in love and concern. Any plan for a church program of discipline must be "a process of reclamation."

5. Before a church develops a program of church discipline, *some prior questions must be considered*. For instance, who is to

take the initiative? In the New Testament examples, discipline was practiced by the church alone. Will this responsibility be handled by the church staff, the deacons, or a standing committee on discipline? The pastor must never assume the role of church disciplinarian.

Where is the church to begin? What particular sins will call for church discipline? Which sins will be handled privately? Or publicly?

Ultimately, each local, autonomous church will have to determine its own policy.

Notes

1. This section on New Testament teachings on growth was adapted from *Salvation in Our Time,* especially the chapter on "Salvation in the Present Tense," pp. 31-33, Lavonn D. Brown. © Copyright 1978 Broadman Press. All rights reserved. Used by permission.

2. Ibid., pp. 35-40.

3. Findley B. Edge, *A Quest for Vitality in Religion,* p. 227.

Bibliography

Dargan, Edwin C. *Ecclesiology: A Study of the Churches.* Louisville: Chas. T. Dearing, 1897.

Edge, Findley B. *A Quest for Vitality in Religion.* Nashville: Broadman Press, 1963.

Foster, Richard J. *Celebration of Discipline.* New York: Harper & Row, 1978.

Hendrix, John and Householder, Lloyd. *The Equipping of Disciples.* Nashville: Broadman Press, 1977.

Howington, Nolan P., McEachern, Alton H., and Pinson, William M. Jr. *Growing Disciples Through Preaching.* Nashville: Broadman Press, 1976.

Marney, Carlyle. *Priests to Each Other*. Valley Forge, Penn.: Judson Press, 1974.

Martin, Ralph P. *The Family and the Fellowship: New Testament Images of the Church*. Grand Rapids, Mich.: Wm. B. Eerdmans, 1980.

McCall, Duke K. *What Is the Church? A Symposium of Baptist Thought*. Nashville: Broadman Press, 1958.

Minear, Paul. *Images of the Church in the New Testament*. Philadelphia: Westminster Press, 1960.

Raines, Robert A. *New Life in the Church*. New York: Harper & Row, 1961.

Southard, Samuel. *Pastoral Evangelism*. Nashville: Broadman Press, 1962.

Thompson, Luther Joe. *Through Discipline to Joy*. Nashville: Broadman Press, 1966.

Trueblood, Elton. *The Incendiary Fellowship*. New York: Harper & Row, 1967.

Part II
The Church:
A Worshiping Community

4

The Essence of Christian Worship

A person can sit through a church service and not have a worship experience. In fact, many do. At times those who plan—or do not plan—the service are to blame. At other times the worshiper must accept responsibility.

Numerous inadequate concepts of worship have developed over the past few years. For many, worship is a filling station where worshipers receive the necessary resources for the "normal" activities of the week. It is little more than the "pause that refreshes."

For others, worship is more like a giant pep rally. Effectiveness seems to be related to the length of prayers, the loudness of the participants, and the fervency of the demonstration. This concept of prayer and worship was vividly illustrated by the 450 prophets of Baal on Mount Carmel (see 1 Kings 18:20-29). They called upon Baal from morning until noon. "And they cried aloud, and cut themselves after their custom with swords and lances, until the blood gushed out upon them. And as midday passed, they raved on until the time of the offering of the oblation, but there was no voice; no one answered, no one heeded" (vv. 28-29).

At any point along the way, the prophets of Baal would have insisted that they were having a great worship experience, while ignoring the question, "Where is the fire?" In contrast, Elijah stepped forward, prayed his brief, confident prayer, "Then the fire of the Lord fell" (v. 38).

Many view worship as something done to us or for us, rather than by us. The pastor or worship leader is the central figure. Worship is a program planned to entertain an audience. The congregation does not need to participate personally.

Perhaps viewing worship as two-way traffic is more accurate. In Jacob's dream at Bethel, "there was a ladder set up on the earth, and the top of it reached to heaven; and behold, the angels of God were ascending and descending on it!" (Gen. 28:12). God's grace and human need intersect in time. Worship is like a stairway set on the ground with its top reaching to the sky. In the moment of worship, God revealed Himself to Jacob, and he responded.

The attitude toward worship and church attendance has radically changed in American life. The typical family is under constant pressure. There is an unparalleled competition for time. Available hours are claimed by a multitude of activities. The result is that our grandfathers called the day for worship holy sabbath. Our fathers called it Sunday. We call it part of the weekend. Our children will probably call it a holiday.

Yet, many people do go to church and will continue to go. Why? Because they are confronted with God in Jesus Christ in worship. They discover new insights into the meaning of life. They find the power needed for Christian living. Multitudes bear burdens from which they might find release through worship. Christian faith must be sustained by regular living encounters with the one true God. In worship the heart is called back to quietness.

The most basic ingredient in Christian worship seems to be the gathering together to celebrate the acts of God in creation and redemption. The assembling together was of major importance (Matt. 18:20; Heb. 10:25). The purpose of worship is to celebrate what God has done, not what we have done. A true celebration must be rooted in an event. In worship we celebrate incarnation, the Christ event. So, worship is a drama reenacting what God has done through Christ.

Worship Defined

Like love, the word *worship* means different things to different people. It has become a catchall word. One might hear it used to describe everything from idolatry to communion with nature from a fishing boat on Sunday morning.

The Idea Within the Word

The evolution of a word is very instructive. The Anglo-Saxon word was *weorthscipe*. The original English word was spelled *worthshippe*, meaning that to which is ascribed highest worth. Worship means worth-ship. In its simplest form, it is the acknowledgment of God's supreme worth. In its broadest sense, worship is the meeting between God and His people.

Is Worship an Obligation or Option?

Numerous Christians consider worship an option. They see it as a possibility but not an obligation. They awaken to a new decision every Sunday morning. To worship or not to worship, that is the question.

Such indecision could be due to an inadequate understanding of worship. If worship is seen as a preaching service, a lecture hall, a psychiatric couch, or show business, then one might conclude that it is an option. However, since worship is the experiencing of divine presence, it is not an option. Many Christians have come to a more adequate definition of worship. For them, worship has become the acknowledgment of God's supreme worth. They worship God because of who He is, not because of what He could do for them. They celebrate God's majesty rather than glorifying themselves. They worship to affirm what God has done, is doing, and will do in their lives. For these Christians worship is an obligation, not an option. It is not always easy. It requires disciplined effort.[1]

When worship is defined as the meeting between God and His people, it becomes essential. Where there is no worship, there is no church because the church is God's people gathered out of the world to celebrate the mighty acts of God in words and deeds.

The Only Worthy Object of Our Worship

Authentic worship must be directed toward God Himself. Worship is a personal meeting with God in which we sing, magnify, and glorify Him for His person and actions. We worship God simply because He is God. None other is worthy. He is the One high, holy, and exalted. He alone is Creator, the Almighty, the King of kings, the Lord of all.

We also worship God because of His gracious acts in history. He entered history and acted in history to redeem and save us. He has promised His faithfulness and love.

In our worship, we adore, praise, and honor God alone. Through our worship, we seek a renewed vision of Him. We begin to interpret life under divine guidance. We celebrate the fact that we are made in His image and, therefore, capable of coming into His presence as persons of worth.

William Temple made a major contribution to our understanding of worship when he said that worship is

> to quicken the conscience of the holiness of God,
> to feed the mind with the truth of God,
> to purge the imagination by the beauty of God,
> to open the heart to the love of God,
> to devote the will to the purpose of God.

All this is gathered up in that emotion which most cleanses us from selfishness because it is the most selfless of all emotions—adoration.[2]

Since it is true that worship is devotion to that which is of supreme worth, then each Christian must ask honestly if God is the object of his or her worship.

Biblical Patterns for Worship

Old Testament Sources

Worship is as old as the human race. It is as universal as it is ancient. Christian worship has its roots in the Old Testament. In fact, descriptions of worship are more common in the Old Testament than the New Testament. God gave His people specific directions regarding the how, when, and where of meeting Him in worship. Some directions carry over into New Testament worship.

Primitive worship.—The Genesis account of beginnings tells of communion between God and the man and woman made in His image. As early as Genesis 4:26, we are told: "At that time men began to call upon the name of the Lord." Also we are introduced to Enoch as one who "walked with God; and he was not, for God took him" (Gen. 5:24). From the very beginning of recorded history, we clearly see traces of worship.

Following the Flood.—After the Flood, "Noah built an altar to the Lord, and took of every clean animal and of every clean bird, and offered burnt offerings on the altar" (Gen. 8:20). That is the first biblical mention of an altar.

Genesis 12:1-3 records God's call of Abraham to go out from his kindred, who were idolaters, and to establish anew the true worship of God. Everywhere Abraham went he built altars and called on the name of the Lord.

Jacob's family worshiped God and sought divine guidance. All through the centuries, God's people have been encouraged by the account of Jacob at the lonely ford of the Jabbok, wrestling all night with the angel of God (see Gen. 32:22-32).

The significance of Sinai.—We may safely assume that the true worship of God was much depressed during the days of Egyptian bondage. When the children of Israel emerged from Egypt under the leadership of Moses, God brought them to Mount Sinai. A public meeting took place between God and Israel at the foot of the mountain (see Ex. 24:1-8 for a full record of the meeting).

Israel received the laws from God concerning their future national life and religious worship. God entered into a covenant relationship with Israel. Moses "took the book of the covenant, and read it in the hearing of the people; and they said, 'All that the Lord has spoken we will do, and we will be obedient'" (v. 7).

To overestimate the significance of Sinai is impossible. The laws and institutions established at the foot of Sinai were the main features of Israel's worship for the rest of Old Testament history.

God on the earth?—The tabernacle and the Temple became the visible and tangible signs of Israel's relationship to God. During the reigns of David and Solomon, the worship of Yahweh had a larger place in the national life than it had ever held before. A major contribution to this new phase of worship was an increased emphasis on music in the worship of David's time. David himself was a great musician. The psalms were set to various melodies and played on different kinds of instruments. Numerous singers were appointed.

The other influence was the removal of the tabernacle to Jerusalem and the building and dedication of the Temple of Solomon. Both the tabernacle and the Temple emphasized the presence of God in the midst of Israel. The establishment of the Temple upon Mount Zion was an event for all the world, for all ages.

Times of transition.—During the time of the divided nation, the prophets emerged as men of great influence in worship. They were the preachers of their age. Exhortation and warning became important elements in the religious life of the people.

After the Exile and during the interbiblical period, the synagogue emerged as the religious, educational, and social center of Jewish village life. Worship in the synagogue was strikingly different from that in the Temple. Synagogue worship consisted of an affirmation of faith (the Shema), prayer, and the Scriptures (the Torah). The sermon interpreted and applied the Scripture reading to the daily life of the people. The influence of the form of synagogue worship on Christian worship was profound. Old Testament principles carried over into Christian worship. The radical differ-

ence was that the event of Jesus Christ became the main content of
Christian worship.

New Testament Developments

The only way to understand worship in the New Testament is to
view it as a process of development. There is no single highly
developed passage on worship in the New Testament. New Testament worship was characterized by variety, flexibility, and movement.

New wine in old wineskins.—The worship of believers described in the New Testament shows a gradual transition from Old
Testament worship styles to that of the Christian church. It is not
exactly like either; yet it is vitally related to both. The movement
was away from the elaborate ritual and sacrificial system of the
Old Testament to the simplicity and spirituality of Christian worship.

The Book of Hebrews describes how the ritualistic forms of the
Old Testament were fulfilled in Christ. Hebrews 13:10-16 reflects
the way the sacrifice of Christ transformed the worship of the Old
Testament and perfected spiritual worship.

> We have an altar from which those who serve the tent have no right
> to eat. For the bodies of those animals whose blood is brought into
> the sanctuary by the high priest as a sacrifice for sin are burned
> outside the camp. So Jesus also suffered outside the gate in order
> to sanctify the people through his own blood. Therefore let us go
> forth to him outside the camp, and bear the abuse he endured. For
> here we have no lasting city, but we seek the city which is to come.
> Through him then let us continually offer up a sacrifice of praise to
> God, that is, the fruit of lips that acknowledge his name. Do not
> neglect to do good and to share what you have, for such sacrifices
> are pleasing to God.

Early Christians worshiped in continuity with the past. At the
same time, the church developed characteristics that were distinct
from Old Testament worship. The separation was gradual. Many
of the elements of synagogue worship were naturally and perma-

nently passed on into the Christian churches and remain a vital part of Christian worship to this day.

Jesus' attitude toward worship.—The followers of Christ must be vitally interested in what He taught and practiced concerning worship. During the transition time, Jesus supported the worship described in the Old Testament. Luke recorded that, on Jesus' arrival in Nazareth, "he went to the synagogue, *as his custom was,* on the sabbath day" (4:16, author's italics). Here we have a flash of insight into the early life of Jesus. He formed the habit of going to public worship as a boy; He kept up the habit as a man.

Jesus saw the Old Testament institutions of worship as pointing to Himself. The sacrifice of Christ on the cross made the sacrificial system of the Old Testament obsolete. Jesus proclaimed the end of Temple worship when He declared that one "greater than the temple is here" (Matt. 12:6).

Jesus prepared the way for the significant changes that occurred in worship when he said, "The sabbath was made for man, not man for the sabbath; so the Son of man is lord even of the sabbath" (Mark 2:27-28). Man existed before the sabbath. A day of worship was God's gift to make life better for man. The Lord of our lives is also Lord of the sabbath. We are directly responsible to Him.

The strongest impression we receive from Jesus is that the worship He encourages should be genuine, simple, and spiritual. To the Samaritan woman He said, "But the hour is coming, and now is, when the true worshipers will worship the Father in spirit and truth, for such the Father seeks to worship him. God is spirit, and those who worship him must worship in spirit and truth" (John 4:23-24).

The worship of the early church.—The New Testament church was a fellowship of believers before it took on organizational form. The first converts to Christianity were Jews. They continued to worship in the Temple (Acts 2:46 to 3:1) and to meet their Jewish brethren in the synagogues (Acts 6:9). This suggests a close alliance between Jewish and Christian worship.

However, tension between the two groups mounted early. Christian worshipers began to gather in private houses, upper rooms, hired dwellings, and in schools. According to Luke, "They devoted themselves to the apostles' teaching and fellowship, to the breaking of bread and the prayers" (Acts 2:42). A Christ-centered content for Christian worship began to develop. The "apostles' teaching" included the life, death, resurrection, and exaltation of Jesus, His enthronement as Messiah, and the hope of His return.

Gradually, the Hellenistic Jews began to renounce Jewish ritualism. For them the Temple had been superseded by the work of Christ. Jewish rituals began to be reinterpreted as having been fulfilled in Christ. For the Hellenist, Jewish and Christian worship did not mix.

Then came the Gentiles.—The conversion of Gentiles brought a new dimension to Christian worship. Many of the Gentiles had come directly out of paganism. They had a limited background in worship, yet were highly interested in maintaining their freedom. The Corinthian letters reveal the disorder and disruption which resulted. Paul found it necessary to emphasize the importance of order. Because Gentile freedom had gotten out of hand, Paul urged that "all things should be done decently and in order" (1 Cor. 14:40). Apparently worship was at times a chaotic mass of confusion.

The four great elements of New Testament worship were prayer (1 Tim. 2:1-2), praise or singing (Eph. 5:19-20; Col. 3:16), the reading of Scripture (1 Tim. 4:13), and teaching or preaching (1 Tim. 4:13-16). These remain the well-established custom of all Christians in all ages and countries. To these must be added the ordinances (baptism and the Lord's Supper) which were probably held in connection with the regular worship.

The Importance of Worship

What is the primary function of the church? In recent years, sincere Christians have had difficulty deciding. The ongoing debate is between evangelism and worship as the church's chief aim. Many have thought these were of equal importance.

W. T. Conner is remembered for his strong statement on worship:

> The first business, then, of a church is not evangelism, nor missions, nor benevolence; it is worship. The worship of God in Christ should be at the center of all else that the church does. It is the mainspring of all the activity of the church. . . . The whole life and organization of a church should spring from worship, center in worship, and end in worship.[3]

David Watson in his book, *I Believe in the Church*, sounded a similar note: "The primary task of the church is to worship God. Even before the obvious evangelistic and missionary work, God's people are called to be a worshipping community."[4]

Worship is to the church like breathing to the human organism; it is an absolute necessity. The church must worship to live. But it must not stop with worship. Worship provides the inspiration for everything else the church does. Evangelism, missions, and other functions of ministry flow from the worship of the church.

If a church only worships, it may become ingrown, live in the past, and traditional. If a church only evangelizes, it may become overactive, formless, and rootless. Worship is kept vital by evangelism, and evangelism is kept orderly by worship. For this reason many have insisted on their equal importance. True worship will keep a church strong in evangelism, missions, and ministry.

The Values of Worship

Each Sunday millions of Americans gather for worship. Each year hundreds of millions of person hours are invested in this unique function of the church. Corporate worship is the local church's central group experience and a major means of communicating the Christian message.

What values come to the worshiper out of this experience? What contribution is made to the quality of life because people have interrupted their daily routine to recognize the supreme worth of God? What difference does worship make in the life of the Christian?

Experiencing the reality of God.—The first value of worship is a close, conscious, personal relationship between God and the worshiper. Worship is an experience of transcendence. This is crucial in an age when technological pursuits have dulled our awareness of the world of wonder and the wisdom of awe. The inner life has been neglected, resulting in inward poverty. When persons can no longer experience wonder, no longer feel amazement, life becomes like a snuffed-out candle.

Worship is a way of renewing one's awareness of the eternal, vertical dimension in the crowded dailyness of time. Experiencing wonder and awe can revive and stretch the spirit of the worshiper. The prophet Isaiah described his life-changing experience of transcendence:

> I saw the Lord sitting upon a throne, high and lifted up; and his train filled the temple. . . . And one [seraphim] called to another and said:
>
>> "Holy, holy, holy is the Lord of hosts;
>> the whole earth is full of his glory."
>
> And the foundations of the thresholds shook at the voice of him who called, and the house was filled with smoke (Isa. 6:1,3-4).

Experiencing the fellowship of human beings.—Worship is a blending of the vertical (person-to-God) and the horizontal (person-to-person). It results in a close, personal relationship both to God and fellow worshipers. People are impelled to worship by a deep desire for togetherness.

Technological advancements, increased mobility, and psychological barriers have caused feelings of isolation, loneliness, and alienation. A woman attending a certain church was asked, after the service, whether she were a stranger there. She responded, "Why, yes, I've been a stranger here for forty years."

Worship is relating. In worship we reverently enter into the lives of other people. Worship brings together those who are "of the same mind, having the same love, being in full accord and of one mind" (Phil. 2:2). In corporate worship, a congregation experiences being drawn together which helps to overcome the shadow of loneliness and isolation. People are lifted out of neurotic self-concern into healthful relationships. Everyone—weak and strong alike—needs meaningful, supportive experiences. We are all empowered by the awareness of belonging.

Experiencing the pursuit of wholeness.—Life easily gets out of focus. Often Christians will take one small segment of life and blow it up as though it were the whole. The most common example is a materialism which assumes that life does, indeed, consist in the abundance of things possessed.

The experience of Christian worship brings wholeness back into the picture. It enriches personality and strengthens character. For many people the worship hour is the only time during the week when they sit quietly and "collect" themselves. There is healing power in quietness and rest. Most worshipers respond to the ancient invitation, "Come to me, all who labor and are heavy laden, and I will give you rest" (Matt. 11:28).

In worship we regain lost perspective. Our sense of values is constantly corrected. Worship gives the individual an opportunity to separate the wheat from the chaff and to recall values the world does not recognize. Without worship life becomes like a movie with the sound track slightly off. The words are not synchronized to lip and body movements. Life never quite makes sense without the worship of God.

Experiencing the redemptive element.—Over against God's holiness stands mankind's sinfulness. Sin is a tragic fact of human experience. Sin and guilt often stand as barriers to fellowship with God and other human beings. Unforgiven sin and unconfessed guilt can corrode the spirit and erode physical health. The psalmist described vividly the effect:

> When I declared not my sin, my body wasted away
>   through my groaning all day long.
> For day and night thy hand was heavy upon me;
>   my strength was dried up as by the heat of summer (Ps.
>   32:3-4).

He also described the joy of deliverance:

> Blessed is he whose transgression is forgiven,
>   whose sin is covered.
> Blessed is the man to whom the Lord imputes no iniquity,
>   and in whose spirit there is no deceit (Ps. 32:1-2).

Worship discloses the ugliness of sin and the need of a Savior. The church must never overlook the seriousness and prevalence of the problems of sin and guilt. In worship Christ must be presented as the one who keeps on cleansing us from all sin. Only then does the sinner find salvation and the Christian experience forgiveness.

Experiencing the replenishing of inner resources.—One of the major values of worship is in the balance of intake and outgo. Worship is a spiritual feeding experience. It helps the worshiper overcome inner emptiness by the periodic replenishing of inner resources.

The spiritual hunger in the world is immense. The church provides nurture for millions. They come to the church's worship to be fed the "bread of life." They hunger and thirst after righteousness, acceptance, love, and strength. In the worship, their spirits are nourished by the hymns and anthems, by the inspiration of great passages from the Bible, by the challenge of a thoughtful sermon, and by the supportive presence of friends.

One of the functions of Christian worship is to help people handle the crises of life. It helps the worshiper face the actual problems and difficulties in the light of Christian faith. Worshipers take their inner struggles, fears, and burdens with them to the worship service. Many find new perspectives and fresh energy for problem solving, load carrying, and burden bearing. Worship will not solve all the Christian's problems. However, without worship multitudes bear burdens from which they might find release through worship.

Unworthy Substitutes for Worship

Nearly all people worship in one way or another. Mankind is made for worship or devotion. In fact, worship is so important to life that, in the absence of the worship of God, people will substitute the worship of something else. One of the proofs of the value of a vital Christian faith is the numerous efforts to find substitutes for its basic disciplines. The empty life will not remain empty. This is reflected in Jesus' eerie little parable:

> When the unclean spirit has gone out of a man, he passes through waterless places seeking rest, but he finds none. Then he says, "I will return to my house from which I came." And when he comes he finds it empty, swept, and put in order. Then he goes and brings with him seven other spirits more evil than himself, and they enter and dwell there; and the last state of that man becomes worse than the first. So shall it be also with this evil generation (Matt. 12:43-45).

Human beings will worship something. If not the true God, then they will begin to ascribe supreme worth to other things. In the Bible, this is called idolatry. Unworthy substitutes may include the worship of self, country, a group of like-minded people, or the forces of nature.

Apparently human beings cannot live for long without the voice of the supernatural. If the Bible is rejected, some other voice will be substituted. Check any bookstore for the abundance of books on the occult, astrology, and the reading of horoscopes. People are capable of communion with God. They long for some word with God. If not through prayer and Christian meditation, then unworthy substitutes will be sought. During the decade of the seventies, Americans flocked into Eastern religions, Transcendental Meditation, and cult and sect movements. People seek out some kind of caring fellowship. If not the church, then some other group will be substituted. Some of these small groups will have religious overtones. Others will be strictly secular adventures. But, people will not live in isolation.

The presence of the counterfeit proves one thing; somewhere the real article exists, otherwise, how could the presence of the counterfeit be explained? There is no worthy substitute for the worship of God.

Toward a Theology for Worship

Worship is something we do. It is human love responding to divine love. It is the creatures' reaction to the Creator's action. Worship is man and woman, created in the image of God, obeying the commandment, "You shall love the Lord your God with all your heart, and with all your soul, and with all your might" (Deut. 6:5). Certain features are essential in Christian worship.

God Is the Object of Our Worship

God does not worship. He is the one worshiped. We worship God simply because He is God. He is high, holy, and lifted up. He alone is God. There is none other besides Him. He is creator of all, and Lord of all. He alone is worthy of our worship. God made us and has redeemed us. We owe him our loyalty, worship, and awe.

Therefore, essential worship must always be directed toward the living God. It is not a performance permitting preachers, musicians, and singers to display their talents before God. Rather, the aim of worship is to glorify God. Worship is to lead worshipers to an increased awareness of His presence in their lives. The hymns, prayers, preaching, and ordinances should all combine to magnify the Lord. In worship we accept the psalmist's invitation, "O magnify the Lord with me, and let us exalt his name together!" (Ps. 34:3).

Christ Is the Center of Our Worship

The events surrounding the life, death, and resurrection of

Jesus Christ are the main content of Christian worship. The prophecies, promises, and ritualistic forms of the Old Testament were fulfilled in Christ. God has come to us in Jesus Christ. Sinful humanity is brought to God by faith in Jesus Christ. The worship of the church is a celebration of redemption brought into the world in Jesus Christ. Consequently, only in and through Christ may we offer our worship.

The Holy Spirit Is the Enabler of Our Worship

The worship of the church is empowered by the Holy Spirit. In worship, the Spirit of God and the spirit of man interact. The essential function of the Spirit in worship, then, is to enable us to worship. Paul wrote that we must "worship by the Spirit of God" (Phil. 3:3, ASV).

Through the Spirit, we have access to God the Father. The Holy Spirit inspires our prayer and praise, opens our minds to spiritual truth, convicts of sin, brings renewal, and bestows spiritual gifts for the common good. He is the breath, life, and enabler of the worshiping community.

Conclusion

Evangelical Christians have viewed worship largely in one of two ways. The role of the congregation provides the key.

In one view of worship, the congregation is largely passive. They are spectators viewing a performance. The assembled people are conceived of as a target group to be taught, persuaded, or even manipulated. The worship leaders on the platform are the performers or actors. God is the prompter in the wings in case the performers forget their lines.

The second model seems to have originated with the Danish philosopher, Søren Kierkegaard. He portrayed the biblical concept of worship as a drama where the congregation is the actor. The preacher, singer, and choir are not the actors; the congregation is! In this view the worship leaders are the prompters. God is the audience. Worship is something done "with" rather than "for" the congregation. The act of worship becomes a celebration of what God is doing among His people.

Notes

1. See Robert Bailey, *New Ways in Christian Worship*, p. 17.
2. William Temple, *The Hope of a New World* (London: The Macmillan Co., Ltd. 1942), p. 30.
3. Walter T. Conner, *The Gospel of Redemption*, pp. 277,279.
4. David Watson, *I Believe in the Church*, p. 179.

Bibliography

Bailey, Robert W. *New Ways in Christian Worship*. Nashville: Broadman Press, 1981.

Carey, John J. *Marney and the Southern Baptists*. Louisville: *Review and Expositor,* Vol. LXXX, No.1, Winter 1983.

Clinebell, Jr., Howard J. *Mental Health Through Christian Community*. Nashville: Abingdon Press, 1965.

Conner, Walter T. *The Gospel of Redemption*. Nashville: Broadman Press, 1945.

Dana, H. E., and Sipes, L. M. *A Manual of Ecclesiology*. Kansas City, Kan.: Central Seminary Press, 1944.

Dargan, Edwin C. *Ecclesiology: A Study of the Churches*. Louisville: Chas. T. Dearing, 1897.

Dobbins, Gaines S. *The Church at Worship*. Nashville: Broadman Press, 1962.

Edge, Findley B. *The Greening of the Church*. Waco: Word Books, 1971.

Martin, Ralph P. *The Family and the Fellowship: New Testament Images of the Church*. Grand Rapids, Mich.: Wm. B. Eerdmans, 1980.

Watson, David. *I Believe in the Church*. Grand Rapids, Mich.: Wm. B. Eerdmans, 1978.

Webber, Robert E. *Worship Is a Verb*. Waco: Word Books, Inc., 1985.
—————————, *Worship Old and New*. Grand Rapids, Mich.: Zondervan, 1982.

5

The Elements of Christian Worship

Someone has suggested that, if Abraham Lincoln had been talking about worship rather than fooling people, his famous statement would have gone like this: "You can prompt some of the people to worship God all of the time, and all of the people some of the time, but you can't prompt all of the people to worship God all of the time." Two people sit in the same worship service yet have completely different experiences. The elements of worship are the same but the responses are totally different.

One wonders if Isaiah were alone in his high hour of worship or if this were a regularly scheduled worship service with others present? Did the other worshipers have the same experience? Or did Isaiah have an experience for which others were not prepared?

> In the year that King Uzziah died I saw the Lord sitting upon a throne, high and lifted up; and his train filled the temple. Above him stood the seraphim; each had six wings: with two he covered his face, and with two he covered his feet, and with two he flew. And one called to another and said:
>
> > "Holy, holy, holy is the Lord of hosts;
> > the whole earth is full of his glory."
>
> And the foundations of the thresholds shook at the voice of him who called, and the house was filled with smoke (Isa. 6:1-4).

Students of worship have discovered all the essential elements of public worship in the sixth chapter of Isaiah. Isaiah's vision in the Temple suggests some important stages through which the worshiper should go. First, Isaiah's heart was prepared for worship. His hero-king was dead. Evidently Isaiah was discouraged, heavyhearted, and in need of help. He went to the Temple, seeking a word from God. Something remarkable took place. A heavenly scene, a renewed vision unfolded before him. Second, he saw the Lord "high and lifted up." God was on His throne in the time of crisis. His royal robe unfolded to fill the hall. Ministering spirits adored Him as the Holy One. In the experience of worship, Isaiah saw things the casual worshiper did not see. In worship there is no substitute for a deep awareness of the reality of God.

Third, Isaiah became aware of personal sin and involvement in the sins of the people of his time. "Woe is me! For I am lost" (v. 5) is the cry of self discovery that follows any true vision of God. Worship involves a deep sense of the awfulness of sin and the need for forgiveness. Fourth, Isaiah experienced cleansing. When the burning coal touched Isaiah's mouth, the seraphim said, "Behold, . . . your guilt is taken away, and your sin forgiven" (v. 7). There is no painless cure for sin. Confession and forgiveness are vital elements of worship.

Fifth, responsibility followed forgiveness. No sooner had Isaiah been forgiven than he heard a voice saying, "Who will go for us?" (v. 8). Could he ignore the voice of God? Having experienced grace, could Isaiah turn his back on his high obligation to God and his responsibility to his people? Finally, the worship experience ended in a high moment of dedication. Isaiah's response to all he had seen and felt was, "Here am I! Send me" (v. 8). In an act of commitment, he offered his whole life as a witness and a service to God. The extent of one's willingness to serve is always a measure of one's gratitude to God for forgiveness.

The Formation of Christian Worship

The order of Christian worship has a biblical basis. Even though there is no model service of worship in the New Testament, most of the elements used in later worship services are there. One of the earliest descriptions of Christian worship is found in Acts

2:42: "And they devoted themselves to the apostles' teaching and fellowship, to the breaking of bread, and the prayers." One is immediately impressed with the devout simplicity of worship in the apostolic age. In the process of development, something happened in worship which caused Paul to emphasize the necessity of order. There was a need to do things in a fitting and orderly way (1 Cor. 14:40).

All Christian worship is based on the biblical record. The Christian faith is sustained by living encounters with the one true God through worship. For that reason, many are rightly disturbed by the sheer chaos of much of our worship. Has worship become a lost art of modern Christianity? Do we have a heritage in worship that needs to be recovered? Perhaps we need a fresh look at the biblical basis and present practice with regard to the elements of Christian worship.

Most Christians would be happy to recreate the beautiful picture of heavenly worship described in Revelation 7:11-12:

> And all the angels stood round the throne and round the elders and the four living creatures, and they fell on their faces before the throne and worshiped God, saying, "Amen! Blessing and glory and wisdom and thanksgiving and honor and power and might be to our God for ever and ever! Amen."

Preparation for Worship

Most people come to the worship service with little preparation. Their lives are rushed and hectic. They bring burdens and needs. At best they are a divided and isolated group of individuals. They need a time of preparation in order to become a worshiping community.

Leaders of worship need time to prepare themselves. In most cases, the congregation will not go beyond those who lead them in worship. A time for prayers, meditation, and discussion prior to the service is essential for worship leaders.

Members of the congregation also need preparation for worship. This preparation generally takes place in stages. It begins as worshipers enter the meeting place and greet one another with friendly smiles and handshakes. Upon finding seats, worshipers can find a moment of prayer and meditation helpful.

Some churches have a brief verbal call to silence. A period of silence before the choir and worship leaders enter helps prepare the worshipers with reverence, awe, openness, and preparation. The prophet Habakkuk captured this feeling when he declared, "The Lord is in his holy temple; let all the earth keep silence before him" (2:20). While silence continues or during an appropriate hymn, the worship leaders and choir enter and take their places. Their entrance should be a signal to the congregation of entering into the very presence of God.

The call to worship, whether sung or spoken, should be carefully selected. It should establish the mood, introduce the theme, and focus attention on the primary purpose of the service. The invocation should be considered a part of preparation for worship. It is addressed to God and invokes His blessing. It should be brief, reverent, and related to the purpose of the service. It may include a confession of corporate sin and a prayer for forgiveness. All these elements of preparation are intended to form the congregation into a worshiping community.

The Elements of Worship

Most of the elements used in present-day worship can be traced back to the synagogue or early church.

The Centrality of the Word

In the basic pattern for worship given in Isaiah 6, a deep awareness of the reality of God preceded the call to discipleship. God takes the initiative in the divine—human encounter. As a rule, revelation precedes response in the worship experience. The first major movement in Christian worship is God speaking through His Word. This communication occurs through the reading of Scripture and the preaching of the sermon.

God speaks through His written Word.—A strong emphasis on

the regular public reading of Scripture was carried directly from the Temple to the synagogues and on into Christian worship. Perhaps the best model is found in Ezra the scribe, as recorded in the Book of Nehemiah:

> And Ezra the scribe stood on a wooden pulpit which they had made for the purpose; . . . and Ezra opened the book in the sight of all the people; and when he opened it all the people stood. And Ezra blessed the Lord, the great God; and all the people answered, "Amen, amen," lifting up their hands; and they bowed their heads and worshiped the Lord with their faces to the ground (Neh. 8:4-6).

An assigned place for the public reading of Scripture was also a regular part of synagogue worship. On one occasion Jesus went to the synagogue in Nazareth. "As his custom was, on the sabbath day. And he stood to read; and there was given to him the book of the prophet Isaiah" (Luke 4:16-17). He opened the scroll, found the place, and read the Scripture lesson. The reading of Scripture was a part of the early churches founded by Paul. " 'Till I come," he advised young Timothy, "attend to the public reading of scripture, to preaching, to teaching" (1 Tim. 4:13). These illustrations demonstrate the supreme value of the content and manner of Scripture reading in public worship.

A surprising trend in many Evangelical churches is the contemporary neglect of the careful reading of Scripture. Study the order of worship in most church bulletins. Missing is any clear evidence of the centrality of the Word in Christian worship. Even less time is given to the reading of Scripture than is given to preaching.

The more liturgical churches usually incorporate a great deal more Scripture in worship than many Evangelicals. We should strive earnestly and faithfully to retrieve what has been neglected. The Bible should be read, not simply as the basis of a sermon, but as God's Word to God's people.

Some churches use a lectionary which is a book that lists different selected Scripture passages for reading in a worship service.

The lectionary provides carefully selected Old and New Testament passages for each Sunday of the year. It is based on a three-year cycle, years A, B, and C. Its purpose is to unfold the full sweep of God's revelation. It is a time-tested antidote for the hit-or-miss methods which plague many pulpits. One who follows the lectionary suggestions is reading out of the wholeness that belongs to the history of the church. Worship planners may wish to become familiar with these readings in giving Scripture its rightful place in the order of worship.

The minister should give careful attention to the public reading of Scripture. Unless the meaning of the passage is clearly understood by the reader, the reading will be done poorly. The Scripture selections should be read and reread with emphasis on oral interpretation. Unfamiliar and difficult words should be checked for correct pronunciation.

For many worshipers, the Scriptures read in church are the only Bible reading for the week. Therefore the passage to be read should be prayerfully chosen and carefully prepared. It need not always be the sermon text for the day, although it is usually related. Responsive or unison readings from the hymnbook are helpful since many worshipers do not bring Bibles or have a variety of translations. The public reading of Scripture should be considered an act of worship. It should be done with simplicity, dignity, and reverence.

God speaks through the spoken word.—Scripture that is read without explanation or interpretation may be ignored or misunderstood. When Ezra the scribe opened the book of the law and read it to the people, he realized that his task was not complete. He enlisted helpers to assist the people in understanding. "They [the helpers] read from the book, from the law of God, clearly; and they gave the sense, so that the people understood the reading" (Neh. 8:8). The purpose of the sermon is to "give the sense" so that the people will understand.

The early New Testament church was unquestionably a preaching church. Many believe that the church as a self-conscious community had its origin on the Day of Pentecost. On that day Peter, speaking and exhorting from Scripture, addressed himself first to the brethren (Acts 1:15-22) and then to the multitude (2:14-36). When they heard that "God has made him both Lord and Christ, this Jesus whom you crucified," they were "cut to the heart" and said, "What shall we do?" (Acts 2:36-37).

The Book of Acts is the account of the spread of the gospel by the preaching of the apostles. Nothing stopped them. Even when the Christians were driven out of Jerusalem through persecution, "those who were scattered went about preaching the word" (Acts 8:4). Numerous New Testament words are used to describe the early Christians' verbal proclamation: they announced, explained, confessed, charged, admonished, rebuked, preached, heralded, testified, taught, exhorted, argued, disputed, confounded, proved, reasoned, persuaded, and pleaded.

Peter listed preaching as a part of the church's task: "But you are a chosen race, a royal priesthood, a holy nation, God's own people, that you may declare the wonderful deeds of him who called you out of darkness into his marvelous light" (1 Pet. 2:9). Paul, the old warrior, "fought the good fight." He was ready to lay his armor aside. Young Timothy, and others like him, would continue the battle. Paul issued the cry to arms: "I charge you in the presence of God and of Christ Jesus who is to judge the living and the dead, and by his appearing and his kingdom: preach the word, be urgent in season and out of season, convince, rebuke, and exhort, be unfailing in patience and in teaching" (2 Tim. 4:1-2).

These biblical references clearly reveal the centrality of preaching as an element of Christian worship. Preaching in itself is an act of worship. Preaching is an offering made to God on behalf of the preacher. Martin Luther regarded the sermon as the very heart of worship. In fact, he suggested that where there is no sermon there is no worship. The gospel is, after all, a personal message borne best by persons. This does not mean that other elements of worship are to be considered preliminaries or as preparatory to worship. It simply means that preaching is crucial.

Many modern-day churches seem to have lost confidence in the proclamation of the Word of God. In the hustle and bustle of ecclesiastic routine, preaching is relegated more and more to the margin of the worship experience. Some ministers seem to have lost confidence in their preaching.

Often the problem is one of lack of preparation. Ministers must have fresh, insightful, stimulating interpretation of God's Word to offer. Their attitude toward preaching should not be like the childhood game of hide-and-seek, "Here I come, ready or not." On one occasion a preacher was told that, if he didn't quit preaching, he would die of a heart attack. He quit for three months but went back to preaching. He explained, "I would rather die preaching than die of listening to some of the stuff I have been hearing." The church of today needs to recover its confidence in the effectiveness of preaching.

Generally speaking, the better the life of the preacher, the greater the fruit produced. The minister is expected to embody the message in his conduct or life-style. There must be no contradiction between words and deeds. Ideally the minister will quench his own spiritual thirst with the Bible. He must live in the house of his own preaching and speak out of his own experience because people still long to hear the Word of God accurately interpreted for them with fresh application for their day. Preaching will continue to be a powerful aid to worship as long as people hear the voice of God speaking to their hearts concerning eternal realities.

The Response of the People

In the worship experience, revelation precedes response. After God has spoken through His written and proclaimed Word, a worthy response may be anticipated. The other elements of worship found in the New Testament are largely related to the response of the people.

Responding through music and praise.—Both vocal and instrumental music are vital to preparation for and participation in worship. Thankfulness to God for His loving, constancy, and caring is expressed through singing, praising, and prayer. Worship and music are inseparable.

Throughout Hebrew history, vocal and instrumental music have been associated with worship. Singing has always been a basic ingredient of praise. The psalmist called on worshipers to "make a joyful noise to God,/ . . . sing the glory of his name;/give to him glorious praise" (66:1). Priest-musicians gave full time to their musical service in the Temple (1 Chron. 15:16). The Book of Psalms has been called the "hymnbook" of Israel. The singing was accompanied by a variety of instruments: trumpets, lutes, harps, timbrels, pipes, and cymbals (Ps. 150:3-5).

The birth of Christ was announced by an outburst of song by the heavenly choir, "praising God and saying, 'Glory to God in the highest, and on earth peace among men with whom he is pleased!'" (Luke 2:13-14). After Jesus instituted the Lord's Supper, Matthew recorded that the service was concluded with the singing of a hymn (Matt. 26:30).

How can we forget those songs of praise at midnight in the inner prison at Philippi? Where did Paul and Silas learn those songs of praise? Such hymns were an accepted and well-established part of the earliest Christian worship. Paul often referred to the importance of singing within the fellowship of the church.

By the time of the prison letters of Paul, a distinction was already being made between different kinds of melodies, but all were considered legitimate means of praise to God. He told the Ephesian Christians to go on "addressing one another in psalms and hymns and spiritual songs, singing and making melody to the Lord with all your heart" (Eph. 5:19). In the Colossian letter, Paul encouraged the believers to "sing psalms and hymns and spiritual songs with thankfulness in your hearts to God" (Col. 3:16). The "psalms" obviously refer to the psalms common to Jewish worship in the tabernacle, Temple, and synagogue. The "hymns" were probably new songs of praise presenting the new Christology. "Spiritual songs" may have used a single word, such as "Alleluia," or may have been chanted in an experience of ecstatic worship.

From the beginning, the Christian faith has been expressed with joyful music that has not been matched by any other religion in history. Some have insisted that more worshipers learn their views of God from music than from sermons. For this reason, hymns and anthems used for public worship should be selected only after prayerful appraisal and careful examination of their wording. Since music can be an asset to every phase of worship, it needs to be theologically sound, suitable for congregational singing, and well performed.

The purpose of music, then, is the same as the purpose of all worship. It is to glorify God and to lead worshipers to an increased awareness of God's presence with His people. Therefore, some sing. Some play instruments. Some listen. But no one escapes the impact of the art of music. Because it is such an integral part of worship, music deserves prayerful preparation.

Responding through prayer.—In worship God speaks to His people through His Word. In turn, the people speak to God through prayer. Robert Williamson clarified this when he wrote that in public worship the minister has a dual office, that of prophet and priest. "As a prophet he reads the Scriptures and preaches the sermon; as a priest he leads the people in prayer and praise. As a prophet he is God's voice speaking to the people; as a priest he is the people's voice speaking to God."[1]

Christians saw in the coming of the Lord a new access to God through Jesus Christ. Jesus prayed often (Luke 6:12; John 14:16); He charged His followers to pray (Matt. 6:5 *ff.*; Mark 14:38); and He responded to their request to teach them to pray (Luke 11:1-2). In fact, the prayer which Jesus taught His disciples to pray may well serve as a guide to both private and public prayer:

> Our Father who art in heaven,
> Hallowed be thy name.
> Thy kingdom come,
> Thy will be done,
>> On earth as it is in heaven.
> Give us this day our daily bread;
> And forgive us our debts,
>> As we also have forgiven our debtors;
> And lead us not into temptation,
>> But deliver us from evil (Matt. 6:9-13).

In the rending of the veil of the Temple, Christians recognized that a new access route to God had been established (Matt. 27:51). With the gift of the Spirit came the possibility of prayer at the deepest possible level.

Paul acknowledged the value of corporate prayer. He described Christians as "those who in every place call on the name of our Lord Jesus Christ, both their Lord and ours" (1 Cor. 1:2). Ephesians 1:3-14 may be an example of the content of the prayers used in the early church's worship. Paul urged the Colossians, "Continue steadfastly in prayer, being watchful in it with thanksgiving; and pray for us also" (Col. 4:2).

In corporate prayer, the minister or layperson becomes the voice of the people as they speak to God. For that reason, public prayer must be taken seriously. The Christian minister should give the same careful preparation to his prayers as he does to his preaching. Laypersons often are more conscientious and careful in their preparation for corporate prayer than ministers. The participation of laypeople as leaders in public worship should be increased.

The pastoral prayer is the time for the minister to care for the congregation, as a shepherd for his sheep, by bringing its needs before God. We are persons created in the image of God. God is a person. Prayer is communion, conversation between persons and the personal God. Therefore, listening is as vital to good communication as talking. The element of silence is important to the worship experience. The congregation worships in silence as the minister voices its prayers to God.

Responding through offerings.—From the beginning of time, people have considered it their duty to offer a portion of their substance to the Divine Being. This concept is reflected in the Jewish sacrificial system and the giving of the tithe as an act of worship. In the Old Testament, God's people learned to worship Him by the sacrifice of their possessions. The offering was a part of Temple and synagogue worship. In worship we are to "ascribe to the Lord the glory due his name; bring an offering, and come into his courts!" (Ps. 96:8).

In the New Testament, the law concerning tithing was a general practice. Jesus assumed that those who came to worship would bring their gifts to the altar (Matt. 5:23). In fact, Jesus had more to say on the right handling of money than on heaven.

Paul organized an offering "for the poor among the saints at Jerusalem" (Rom. 15:26). He challenged the members of the church in Corinth to "excel in this gracious work also" (2 Cor. 8:7). The writer of Hebrews urged, "Do not neglect to do good and to share what you have, for such sacrifices are pleasing to God" (13:16).

In the worship of the early church, the offering was a central part. The bringing of tithes and offerings to the place of worship was a specific, deliberate act of worship. It symbolized the self-giving of the worshiper of God.

In the modern-day church, God is still worshiped through the giving of possessions and money. The offering is an act in which every worshiper can participate. It is an expression of worship through which we respond to God's claim on our lives as ultimate owner. It should be done, therefore, with dignity and thankfulness of heart.

Responding through commitment.—The final and definitive test of the effectiveness of our worship is submission. In the stages of worship experienced by Isaiah, a high moment of dedication came as the climax. Having been forgiven, he heard the call of God,

"Who will go for us?" With eagerness and anticipation Isaiah responded, "Here am I! send me." Worship ended with a total commitment of self to the service of God.

Early heralds of the gospel expected something to happen as a result of their preaching. In the first eleven chapters of Paul's Letter to the Romans, he outlined in considerable detail the amazing mercies of God. Only then did he call for commitment: "I appeal to you therefore, brethren, by the mercies of God, to present your bodies as a living sacrifice, holy and acceptable to God, which is your spiritual worship" (12:1). On the Day of Pentecost, an opportunity was offered for specific dedication and commitment on the part of the worshipers.

Churches handle the time of dedication and commitment in a variety of ways. Churches in the Evangelical tradition generally sing a hymn of invitation. Worshipers are invited to respond to the call of Christ for salvation or to join the local fellowship of believers. However, commitment is much broader. Everyone is expected to respond in some way to the Word of God.

Conclusion

The Christian faith is sustained by worship. Both the leaders of worship and the congregation need adequate preparation. Evangelical churches need a genuine renewal of interest in worship. Time could be spent profitably in the study of worship and the education of the people in worship. Care must be taken to orient worship toward the praise of God's person and work rather than toward human beings.

Worship includes both the centrality of the Word and the response of the people. Many churches could benefit by giving more attention to the response of the people. The full congregation should be involved in worship. Those who plan worship must watch for every opportunity to involve laypeople in Scripture reading, drama, music, prayer, and varied ways of serving and receiving the Lord's Supper.

Note

1. Robert L. Williamson, *Effective Public Prayer*, p. 3.

Bibliography

Bailey, Robert W. *New Ways in Christian Worship*. Nashville: Broadman Press, 1981.

Bonhoeffer, Dietrich. *Life Together*. San Francisco: Harper & Row, 1954.

Brown, Robert McAfee. *The Significance of the Church*. Philadelphia: 1956.

Dana, H. E. *A Manual of Ecclesiology*. Kansas City, Kan.: Central Seminary Press, 1944.

Dobbins, Gaines S. *The Church at Worship*. Nashville: Broadman Press, 1962.

Hinson, E. Glenn. *The Integrity of the Church*. Nashville: Broadman Press, 1978.

Hustad, Donald P. *Jubilate! Church Music in the Evangelical Tradition*. Carol Stream, Ill.: Hope Publishing Company, 1981.

Review and Expositor, Vol. LXXX, No.1. (Winter,1983). Louisville: The Southern Baptist Theological Seminary, 1983.

Watson, David. *I Believe in the Church*. Grand Rapids, Mich.: Wm. B. Eerdmans, 1978.

Webber, Robert E. *Worship Is a Verb*. Waco, Tex.: Word Books, Inc., 1985.

_____. *Worship Old and New*. Grand Rapids, Mich.: Zondervan Publishing, 1982.

Williamson, Robert L. *Effective Public Prayer*. Nashville: Broadman Press, 1960.

6

The Ordinances in Christian Worship

Jesus swept away the elaborate rituals of Judiasm but retained two ceremonial ordinances for perpetual observance. They are pictorial representations of the fundamental facts of the gospel. The baptistry and the Lord's Supper table form a backdrop for a symbolic drama. The drama has two acts. Each act reveals things worth remembering about the life, ministry, death, and resurrection of Jesus Christ. Both are rich in spiritual content.

Baptism is a sign that *one is starting out* on a new spiritual journey. It symbolizes belief in the death, burial, and resurrection of Jesus Christ and the convert's death, burial, and resurrection with Him.

The Lord's Supper is a sign of the Christian's *being on the way*. It symbolizes Jesus' shed blood and broken body. In the memorial supper, the believer's past and future are simultaneously made present. The Lord's Supper is intended as a continuing reminder of the price paid for our salvation; also it should be a declaration of renewed dedication to Christ.

Thus the two ordinances set forth in pictorial drama the two basic truths of Christianity, resurrection and atonement, the cross and the empty tomb. They are rightly called *ordinances,* a term which stresses that these acts are ordained by the Lord and appointed to be practiced continually in the church.

The Ordinance of Baptism

We are amazing composites of the accumulation of our choices at significant times in our lives. We are creatures of choice. Time and again, we find ourselves standing at some intersection or fork of the road, asking what we should do, forever after wondering what would have happened if we had chosen the other way. Jesus came to many such turning points in life. One was baptism.

New Testament Teachings on Baptism

John the Baptist broke four hundred years of prophetic silence. He preached, "Repent, for the kingdom of heaven is at hand" (Matt. 3:2). A constant stream of repentant sinners went to the Jordan river to be baptized by John. He preached "a baptism of repentance for the forgiveness of sins" (Luke 3:3). Baptism did not automatically convey that forgiveness. Rather, once a sinner had repented and received forgiveness, baptism was a proper acknowledgment.

The baptism of Jesus.—Basically, the life of Jesus is divided into two parts. Thirty years of privacy and preparation were followed by about three years of public ministry. Between these periods came the significant ceremony of baptism.

> Then Jesus came from Galilee to the Jordan to John, to be baptized by him. John would have prevented Him, saying, "I need to be baptized by you, and do you come to me?" But Jesus answered him, "Let it be so now; for thus it is fitting for us to fulfil all righteousness." Then he consented (Matt. 3:13-15).

Why did Jesus submit to the baptism of John? John's baptism was a call to repentance and an acknowledgment of sin forgiven. Jesus needed neither. However, Jesus had good reasons to be baptized. By submitting to John's baptism, Jesus approved of John's ministry, identified Himself with the people in their movement toward God, and fulfilled a desire to do everything that was right (v. 15). Apparently water baptism was necessary to perfectly complete Jesus' being and doing right. His baptism also launched His public ministry.

Baptism as commanded of Jesus' followers.—John recorded that "Jesus and his disciples went into the land of Judea; there he remained with them and baptized" (John 3:22). The time came when greater crowds came to Jesus than to John to be baptized. A note of explanation was added: "Jesus himself did not baptize, but only his disciples" (4:2). Apparently Jesus agreed to this practice of baptism.

Jesus was baptized by John. He agreed that the disciples should baptize believers and commissioned the disciples to baptize. At the close of Jesus' physical ministry, He gave "marching orders" to the New Testament church. His instructions were to go and make disciples of all nations, "baptizing them in the name of the Father and of the Son and of the Holy Spirit" (Matt. 28:19). Baptism was to be followed by careful instruction in Christian living (v. 20). Christian baptism is certainly believed to be commanded by Jesus.

Baptism as practiced by the early church.—Baptism was not just an individual act concerning only Christ and the person baptized. In the early church, baptism was the outward sign of admission to the Christian fellowship.

After Peter's sermon on the day of Pentecost, "those who received his word were baptized, and there were added that day about three thousand souls" (Acts 2:41). This was the church in a formative stage. Luke continued, "And the Lord added to their number day by day those who were being saved" (v. 47). Through baptism the believer becomes a member of the community which, as a whole, owes its allegiance to Jesus.

The Meaning of Baptism

Every aspect of baptism has been debated through the centuries. The proper mode, candidate, and administrator have been discussed. However, little emphasis has been placed on the meaning of baptism for those who submit to it. What is the purpose or significance of baptism?

Following the example of Jesus.—For most Christians, the fact that Jesus was baptized is the significance of baptism. Jesus approved the baptismal activity of the disciples. Christians look to

Jesus as primary example. Baptism is a part of what it means to follow Him.

Obedience to a command.—For many Christians, the sole reason for baptism is the command of Jesus to baptize. Baptism is nothing more than following out the demand of Jesus. It is not logical that we would accept Jesus' lordship and refuse our first opportunity to obey. If the primary motivation is obedience, then meaning and purpose are secondary.

Symbol of identification with Christ.—New converts were baptized "in the name of Jesus Christ" (Acts 2:38). Baptism in the name of a person signified that one belonged to that person. When the name of Jesus was invoked in baptism, the new convert became the possession of Christ. The new believer became clearly identified with Christ in a Master-servant relationship.

Baptism points back in time to the death, burial, and resurrection of Jesus. Each baptism is a commemoration of these central affirmations of the Christian faith. Baptism symbolizes a salvation that comes by faith in Christ.

The significance of Christian baptism for Paul was closely related to union with Christ. The classical source of information is given in Romans 6:1-14. For Paul salvation came, not by human achievement, but by faith. Therefore baptism, by its very symbolism, condemns the idea that one should go on sinning in order that grace may abound. Baptism, according to Romans 6, means the reenactment of what happened to Christ.

> Do you not know that all of us who have been baptized into Christ Jesus were baptized into his death? We were buried therefore with him by baptism into death, so that as Christ was raised from the dead by the glory of the Father, we too might walk in newness of life. For if we have been united with him in a death like his, we shall certainly be united with him in a resurrection like his (vv. 3-5).

A drama of the Christian's experience.—Baptism also pictures the present experience of the believer. Baptism symbolizes death to sin, burial with Christ, and resurrection to walk a new life with Him.

Baptism may be considered a part of the new convert's public testimony of faith in Christ. When the believer walks down into the baptismal waters, he is saying, "I have died to an old, sinful way of life." When he is placed beneath the water, he is saying, "I am being buried to the old way of life." Then, as he is raised out of the water, he is saying, "I am being raised to walk in a completely new life with Christ."[1]

Baptism, then, is an outward symbol of an inward experience. Unless the person being baptized has had the inner experience, baptism is robbed of its meaning. Faith leads to baptism, not baptism to faith. No one has ever been saved without faith; many have been saved without baptism.

Baptism has the practical significance of picturing the renouncing of the old life of sin and the initiation of a new life in Christ. It shows the Christian's liberation from the old sphere in the flesh and entrance into the sphere of Christ. In New Testament writings, this practical significance was often depicted by the metaphor of clothing. The apostle Paul used the figure of clothing in Colossians 3:5-17, which was written in the context of baptism. He named certain things that should be "put off" and certain things that should be "put on." Christians should put off the old clothes of the old life and put on the new clothes which correspond to the character of Christ.

A symbol of union with other believers.—For Paul baptism gave tangible form to Christ's fellowship of believers. Also baptism was a symbol of the unity of believers in Christ. "One baptism" was a part of the sevenfold unity of the Christian fellowship (Eph. 4:5). In Christ all racial and social differences are erased; all humanity becomes one. "For by one Spirit we were all baptized into one body—Jews or Greeks, slaves or free—and all were made to drink of one Spirit" (1 Cor. 12:13).

In the New Testament, baptism was viewed as the effective symbol for binding people into the unity of the Christian fellowship. Through baptism Christians are all made one in Christ. Paul wrote to the Galatians, "For as many of you as were baptized into Christ have put on Christ. There is neither Jew or Greek, there is neither slave nor free, there is neither male nor female; for you are all one in Christ Jesus" (3:27-28).

By baptism we become identified with all believers in their movement toward God. Baptism is our badge of identification, a uniform we wear. C. S. Lewis in *Surprised by Joy* told how, after he came to believe in God, he felt compelled to identify with his parish church. He did so even though the idea of churchmanship was at the time "wholly unattractive" to him. Why, then, did he identify? He explained, "Because I thought one ought to 'fly one's flag' by some unmistakable overt sign."[2] Baptism provides the Christian that opportunity.

The Mode of Baptism

Since the apostolic age, three basic modes of baptism have been widely practiced—sprinkling, pouring, and immersion. Some people who readily grant that the New Testament way of baptizing was by immersion, still argue that there is no necessity for following the New Testament example in the matter. Those churches which continue to follow the New Testament practice do so for many reasons.

The first reason for practicing baptism by immersion has to do with the meaning of the Greek word used for baptism in the New Testament. The word *baptizein,* according to the Greek lexicons, means to dip, plunge, submerge, or immerse. Most Christian scholars agree that New Testament baptism was by immersion. Classical Greek used the word *baptizein* to describe a ship sinking into the sea.

A second reason for baptism by immersion is that the description of baptism, as practiced in New Testament times, suggests immersion. The Gospel of Mark records this account of the baptism of Jesus by John in the Jordan river: "And when he came up out of the water, immediately he saw the heavens opened" (1:10).

We are told in John 3:23 that John was baptizing at Aenon "because there was much water there." Apparently John needed a place with an abundant water supply for baptism. Also, the record of Philip baptizing the eunuch is a clear description of immersion: "They both went down into the water, . . . and he baptized him. And when they came up out of the water, the Spirit of the Lord caught up Philip; and the eunuch saw him no more, and went on his way rejoicing" (Acts 8:38-39).

The final reason for baptism by immersion is a logical one having to do with the meaning of the symbolism behind baptism. Baptism symbolizes death, burial, and resurrection (see Rom. 6:2-4). Only immersion fully accomplishes this symbolism. Can the mode be changed without changing the meaning?[3]

The Candidate for Baptism

Careful study shows a regular New Testament order that repeated itself: (1) an individual heard the gospel, (2) accepted its message, (3) believed in Christ as Savior, and (4) was baptized. The chronology of the Great Commission presents the same order: first we are to "make disciples," "baptizing them," and "teaching them" to live the Christian life (see Matt. 28:19-20). John the Baptist demanded fruit worthy of repentance before He would baptize those who went to him (see Matt. 3:7-8). On the Day of Pentecost, those who "received his word" were baptized (Acts 2:41).

According to New Testament practice, only confessed believers are proper subjects for baptism. When baptism is related to the whole process of salvation, the focus falls on the primacy of faith. Without the exercise of faith, the baptismal act has no validity. Baptism cannot be without faith. For this reason, recent theologians are viewing the baptism of infants as problematic for the church. They are concerned that the practice has perpetuated an involuntary identification with the church from generation to generation.[4]

Some Christian bodies believe that newborn infants are kept under the protective grace of God until an age of accountability or responsibility. At such time, the child can make a personal decision to be a follower of Christ. When the child is old enough to decide for himself, he is also old enough to be baptized by immersion. The meaning and symbolism of baptism also are retained in this way.[5]

The Ordinance of the Lord's Supper

The second act in the church's symbolic drama of Christianity is the Lord's Supper. Its purpose is to reveal some things worth remembering about the death of Christ for a world's sin. When the gospel is preached, we have only the dimension of hearing. Baptism adds the dimension of sight. The Lord's Supper is a powerful aid to Christian memory because it adds the dimensions of touching and tasting to that of hearing and seeing. An ancient Chinese proverb says, "I hear and I forget; I see and I remember; I do and I understand."

New Testament Teachings on the Lord's Supper

What the Passover is to the Old Covenant the Lord's Supper is to the New.

Instituted by Jesus Himself.—Toward the end of Jesus' public ministry, He observed the Passover meal with His disciples in the upper room in Jerusalem. The shadow of the cross fell across the table. Jesus would go from the upper room to Gethsemane to Golgotha. The Last Supper became the major source for the institution of the Lord's Supper (see Matt. 26:26-29).

After the first observance of the supper, according to Paul, Jesus urged His followers to continue the practice, "Do this in remembrance of me" (1 Cor. 11:24). "Do this for my recalling" has been suggested as a more accurate translation.

Interpreted by Paul.—The most extensive discussion of the Lord's Supper is given in 1 Corinthians 11:17-34. Paul's account of the first observance is the earliest written record we possess.

> For I received from the Lord what I also delivered to you, that the Lord Jesus on the night when he was betrayed took bread, and when he had given thanks, he broke it, and said, "This is my body which is for you. Do this in remembrance of me." In the same way also the cup, after supper, saying, "This cup is the new covenant in my blood. Do this, as often as you drink it, in remembrance of me." For as often as you eat this bread and drink the cup, you proclaim the Lord's death until he comes (1 Cor. 11:23-26).

Paul was not an innovator with regard to the Lord's Supper. He made it clear that he was delivering to the Corinthians only what he had "received" (v. 23). He was continuing what had become the established ordinance of the church.

Most Lord's Supper observances are modeled after the service Jesus shared with His disciples. First, "the Lord Jesus . . . took bread" (v. 23), in the same way the minister and celebrants take the bread and the fruit of the vine that are offered. This action signifies the involvement of the whole worshiping community.

Next, Jesus gave thanks (v. 24). Praying a blessing over the bread and fruit of the vine was a universally accepted practice of the ancient church. Thanksgiving is commonly found in contemporary observances. In fact, the service is often called the Eucharist, from the Greek word for *thanksgiving*.

After Jesus gave thanks, He broke the bread (v. 24). This serves as a reminder that Jesus' body was sacrificed on the church's behalf. The same thing is dramatized by the pouring of the fruit of the vine, representing Christ's blood poured out on our behalf. In order to retain this powerful symbolism, even though individual servings of the elements are passed, the minister may want to actually break a loaf of bread and fill his cup before inviting the celebrants to eat and drink.

Finally, Jesus gave the bread and wine to His followers, inviting them to "Take, eat" (Matt. 26:26). At this point, worship becomes a communion. It is a sacred moment. Unfortunately, in the history of the church, this ordinance has been the subject of much controversy as to its meaning and its observance.

Four Distinct Views of the Lord's Supper

Christian history reveals four distinct theories concerning the meaning of the Lord's Supper. The controversy revolves around the manner in which Christ is present in the supper.

Transubstantiation.—According to this view, when the priest consecrates the elements of the supper, they are actually changed into the substance of the flesh and blood of Christ. Although the appearance and taste remain the same, those who partake are eating the flesh and drinking the blood of Christ. The words "This is my body" and "This is my blood" are taken literally. Because the real body of Christ is offered, participation is considered a means of securing God's favor. This view was proclaimed a dogma in the Roman Catholic Church in 1215.

Consubstantiation.—This view denies the change of the substance of the elements while affirming that Christ is bodily present "in, with, and under" the substance of bread and wine. Martin Luther, the originator of this view, insisted on the real and physical presence of Christ in the supper. According to Luther, the body and blood of Christ are mystically and invisibly united with the elements.

The mystical presence.—In John Calvin's Reformed theology, the bodily presence of Christ is denied while the dynamic or spiritual presence is affirmed. Christ is actually present in the elements in such a way that a special divine influence radiates from them. This spiritual presence is different from any other spiritual presence of Jesus. For this reason, a definite spiritual blessing (grace) comes to the believer in the observance of the Lord's Supper which is not available otherwise.

The symbolic meaning.—According to John Zwingli, the elements are symbols of the broken body and spilled blood of Jesus. Therefore, when Jesus said, "This is my body," and "This is my blood," He was speaking symbolically—not literally. These statements would be interpreted in the same way we interpret other statements made by Jesus, such as: "I am the bread of life" (John 6:35), "I am the true vine" (15:1), and "I am the door" (10:7). Jesus was saying that the elements of the supper represent, picture, or symbolize His body and blood.

This view does not deny the presence of Christ in the supper. After all, Jesus promised His followers, "I am with you always, to the close of the age" (Matt. 28:20). Jesus said it was to our advantage that He go away because, in His going, He would send the Holy Spirit, "to be with you for ever" (John 14:16). The living presence of Christ is continually with us in the form of the Holy Spirit. Christ is spiritually present with us as we participate in the supper.

In many churches the observance of the Lord's Supper needs to be revitalized. This powerful teaching drama contains dynamic symbols which hold tremendous potential for Christian living. The observance of the Lord's Supper can be a spiritual blessing for believers. Believers can be strengthened by participation.

The Significance of the Supper

Many Christians have discovered new meaning in the Lord's Supper by considering the various dimensions of its message.

The supper's past significance.—Jesus instituted the supper to preserve for all Christians an authentic memory of His sufferings. The Lord's Supper is a continuing proclamation of a past event: "For as often as you eat this bread and drink the cup, you proclaim the Lord's death until he comes" (1 Cor. 11:26). The Christian is called first to *look back*.

The Lord's Supper receives its meaning from the past. Apart from the past deed—Christ's death on the cross—the present memorial would be emptied of its meaning. Paul recorded the words of Jesus, "Do this in remembrance of me" (1 Cor. 11:24).

While observing the Lord's Supper, we remember how deeply

God cares for us. We remember what unchecked sin can do. We remember that God "did not spare his own son but gave him up for us all" (Rom. 8:32). The Lord's Supper, then, recollects a past event which becomes a present reality in Christian worship.

The supper's present significance.–The observance of the Lord's Supper provides *a recurring opportunity for self-examination.* Paul offered a solemn warning to the Corinthians: "Let a man examine himself, and so eat of the bread and drink of the cup. For any one who eats and drinks without discerning the body eats and drinks judgment upon himself" (1 Cor. 11:28-29). Careless communion results in spiritual weakness. A flippant approach to the supper ignores its greatest potential for the present—self-examination.

We must observe the Lord's Supper again and again because of our periodic need for self-examination and confession. When we go for a physical examination, the doctor is interested in "silent" symptoms, every evidence of unhealth, the absence of wholeness. The Lord's Supper may be a time of spiritual examination. We bring all that we know about ourselves and place it before all that we know about God in Christ. Some questions help our spiritual examination: How am I doing? What is my true spiritual condition? Where are the areas that need forgiveness, growth, healing? Am I in communion with God? Am I in fellowship with other believers?

Believers can eat and drink in an unworthy manner (1 Cor. 11:27). While perfection is not expected or attainable, hatred, bitterness, and unforgiving spirits are not appropriate at the Lord's table.

The observance of the Lord's Supper also provides *a recurring opportunity for participation in fellowship*. Paul was concerned that divisions arising out of class distinctions would destroy the fellowship of the church (1 Cor. 11:17-34). Such actions disgraced the church. The emphasis on the Lord's Supper as a time of fellowship rescues it from the unimportance to which many relegate it. The Lord's Supper is not a solitary meal for the individual but a community meal held in an atmosphere of love—a simplified love feast.

The supper's future significance.—In the Lord's Supper, the church *looks toward the future* with hope: "For as often as you eat this bread and drink the cup, you proclaim the Lord's death *until he comes*" (1 Cor. 11:26, author's italics). We gain assurance from the promise of Christ's return and the knowledge that He is the ultimate Victor. We look forward to the consummation of our salvation, when the returning Lord shall appear in power and great glory.

According to the Synoptic Gospels, Jesus will "not drink again of the fruit of the vine until that day when I drink it new in the kingdom of God" (Mark 14:25; see Matt. 26:29; Luke 22:18). In the observance of the supper, believers look toward the future and a more perfect fellowship. When the kingdom of God is ultimately established, Jesus and His followers will drink the fruit of the vine together again at the messianic banquet. Even so, come, Lord Jesus!

Conclusion

After Jesus' death, two people walked from Jerusalem to Emmaus. Along the way a stranger joined them. At supper that evening, the stranger "took the bread and blessed, and broke it, and gave it to them" (Luke 24:30). They had seen another handle bread in that way. In fact, they had never known anyone to handle a commonplace piece of bread with such wonder and gratitude. So "their eyes were opened and they recognized him," and "he was known to them in the breaking of the bread" (vv. 31,35).

The ordinances were instituted by Jesus to provide an authentic memory of the heart of the gospel. They are sermons in symbols. Baptism reminds us of the death, burial, and resurrection of Jesus. It is an initial act, administered at the beginning of the Christian experience. The Lord's Supper helps us remember the sacrifice of

Jesus on the cross. It is a continuing reminder, observed again and again throughout the Christian's life.

Each time we participate in or observe these ordinances, our eyes are opened again and we recognize Him. He becomes known to us again in the baptismal waters and the breaking of the bread.

Notes

1. Lavonn D. Brown, *Truths that Make a Difference,* p. 108.
2. C. S. Lewis, *Surprised by Joy* (New York: Harcourt Brace Jovanovich Press, 1955), p. 233.
3. Brown, pp. 109-10.
4. Jürgen Moltmann, *Hope for the Church* (Nashville: Abingdon, 1979), p. 47.
5. Brown, pp. 110-11.

Bibliography

Brown, Lavonn D. *Truths that Make a Difference*. Nashville: Broadman Press, 1980.
Conner, W. T. *Christian Doctrine*. Nashville: Broadman Press, 1937.
Dana, H. E. *A Manual of Ecclesiology*. Kansas City, Kan.: Central Seminary Press, 1944.
Guthrie, Donald. *New Testament Theology*. England: Inter-Varsity Press, 1981.
McCall, Duke K. *What Is the Church?* Nashville: Broadman Press, 1958.
Moltmann, Jürgen. *The Church is the Power of the Spirit*. New York: Harper & Row, 1977.
Watson, David. *I Believe in the Church*. Grand Rapids, Mich.: Wm. B. Eerdmans Publishing, 1978.
Webber, Robert E. *Worship Old and New*. Grand Rapids, Mich.: Zondervan Publishing, 1982.

Part III
The Church:
A Serving Community

7

Ministers and the Gifts for Ministry

In the beginning, "The earth was without form and void" (Gen. 1:2). So was the primitive church. Jesus began by calling a group of followers. They were the church in miniature. Before Christ's death, the church existed in bud only. Pentecost was the critical event which empowered the church for its mission and ministry.

As far as church organization is concerned, the primitive church had no consistent pattern of church life. As one reads progressively through the New Testament, the church begins to take on dimension and organization (Acts 20:17-37). And that organization was dynamic, not static.

From the beginning, the church had leaders. On their first missionary tour, Paul and Barnabas "appointed elders for them in every church" (Acts 14:23). The elders of the church in Ephesus were charged: "Take heed to yourselves and to all the flock, in which the Holy Spirit has made you overseers, to care for the church of God which he obtained with the blood of his own Son" (Acts 20:28).

The house churches described in the Book of Acts portray a structure that was loose, flexible, and without form. The churches were more living organisms than organizations. The structures of the early church varied and remained adaptable to the demands of the mission. The modern-day church faces the problem of distinguishing between what the early church did to meet the needs of their time and the timeless principles that guided their actions. For

118

this reason, the study of church officers and church polity (see next chapter) has been called "the battlefield of the giants."

The Earliest Stages of Organization

Three periods of the church's life have been identified. These early stages of organizational development have been compared to bud, blossom, and fruit.[1]

The Bud Stage

In the beginning, the church had no formal organization. The seed of the gospel was still taking root. The church was still vitally connected to the bodily presence of Christ. Jesus was carefully planting teachings in the lives of those who followed Him.

At first the Christian community took on the form of a family. Jesus inspired a growing sense of relationship between Himself and His followers. The power of this newly awakened fellowship began to take precedence in the followers lives.

The Blossom Stage

The church, immediately after Christ's ascension, was under the tutelage of the apostles. They told others about Jesus through preaching and teaching. As a qualified band of eyewitnesses, they were irreplaceable. They filled a unique place in the continuity of faith from Jesus to later generations. Their writings which became the New Testament were eyewitness accounts of their experiences. The apostles prepared the church, by a process of education, for her independence and self-government apart from Judaism.

The Fruit Stage

Since the time of the apostles, the church has borne fruit. As the church grew, she was guided toward a plan for organization and Christian work. The church continues in this fruit-bearing stage. Throughout this stage, the church has had to define her purpose and mission and organize to fulfill its responsibility to her Lord. Doctrines have been developed and church offices established to guide the church on mission. This period of maturing needs further development.

Some General Church Officers

One of the earliest and most obvious distinctions made in the New Testament is between local and itinerant ministries. Certain officers served in a general missionary capacity, going from place to place, as needs demanded. These general officers had no permanent relationship to any particular church. Rather, they traveled from church to church as representatives or ambassadors of Christ for the purpose of establishing churches or encouraging new Christians in their faith. Two offices seem to belong exclusively to the apostolic age and are not essential to the ongoing ministry of the church: apostles and prophets. Two other offices—evangelists and teachers and preachers—seem to belong to this itinerant style of ministry. Even though they had no permanent relationship to any particular church, their ministries have outlived the apostolic age.

Apostles

The term *apostle* was a Greek term which meant messenger or emissary. An apostle was one sent out with a message.

The New Testament apostles shared in four privileges which gave them their place of prominence in the early church:
   (1) They were close companions with Jesus in the days of His flesh (Mark 3:14);
   (2) They saw Christ after His resurrection (Acts 1:21-22; 1 Cor. 9:1);
   (3) They had been commissioned by Jesus Himself to preach (Mark 3:14-15; Gal. 1:1); and
   (4) They had been given authority to perform supernatural deeds (Mark 3:14-15; 2 Cor. 12:12).
Since these last three privileges were shared with others, the first was in its nature incommunicable. There is no hint in Scripture that the apostles appointed successors for the continuation of the

office after their departure. When those who had known Jesus in the days of His flesh died, the designation assumed a different significance.

Prophets

The early Christian prophets, like their counterparts in the Old Testament, were gifts of God to the church at large. They possessed the gift of divinely inspired insight into religious truth. At times this included the supernatural power for discerning the purposes of God concerning future events (Acts 11:28; 21:10-11). Generally, however, their function was inspired, intelligible preaching intended both for the conversion of the unbeliever and for the growth in holiness and knowledge of the individual members of the church (Acts 15:32). As such, prophecy was more a gift than an office.

This office was temporary. The source of authority for Christianity deliberately began to shift toward the Old Testament Scriptures and the writings of the apostles. The result was a gradual change of attitude toward the function of the prophets.

Evangelists

The word *evangelist* occurs only three times in the New Testament. It appears in the list of officers given in Ephesians 4:11. Philip is designated by the name "the evangelist" in Acts 21:8. Young Timothy was exhorted to "do the work of an evangelist" in addition to his other responsibilities (2 Tim. 4:5).

The evangelist was probably a traveling preacher who delivered the first news of the gospel message. The word denotes function rather than a definite office. The Greek verb from which the name comes means to spread the gospel. Hence, the evangelist was a traveling missionary who usually took the good news into territory where it had not previously been heard. The New Testament concept corresponds more to pioneer mission work than to those who make occasional trips for brief revival meetings.

Teachers and Preachers

The church at Antioch had both prophets and teachers (Acts 13:1). Along with other specific gifts, Paul indicated that God had appointed teachers in the church (1 Cor. 12:28). Paul considered himself appointed as "a preacher and apostle and teacher" (2 Tim. 1:11). The writer of Hebrews suggested that, considering the length of time they had been Christians, his readers should have become teachers (Heb. 5:12).

Teachers were charged with training the new converts for church membership. Their function was to interpret the inspired revelation and apply it to the needs of common life. All those gifted in public instruction were set apart to it.

The words *teacher* and *preacher,* like the word *evangelist,* denote primarily a function rather than an office. They had no official authority in the church as church officers. These functions were often joined with other offices.

Local Church Officers

In the period covered by New Testament literature, no hierarchy of ecclesiastical officials developed. However, two officers were related distinctively to the local church and chosen by the local church. Their qualifications and duties were more carefully set out. They were pastors (bishops, elders) and deacons.

The offices of pastor and deacon seem to have developed out of the distinct kinds of work the church began to do. Each congregation began to develop some regular program of worship, teaching, and service ministries. As those ministries began to crystallize into categories, the persons responsible became "officers" of the church.

Pastors (Bishops, Elders)

The words *pastor, bishop, elder* are used interchangeably to describe one office in Scripture. However, considering them separately may be helpful.

Elder.—The word *elder* is used seventeen times in the New Testament. In fact, this term is by far the most frequently used to describe the pastoral function. The first Jewish converts to Christianity continued as active participants in their synagogues. The synagogue had a council of older men, qualified by their years of knowledge and wisdom, who presided over worship. The Jewish reverence for age was naturally carried over into the new Christian community. The appointing of elders from among the older men to care for the church was a natural effort to bring order, wisdom, and maturity to the young congregations.

The development of the office of elder is directly due to the mission and work of the early church. In the early chapters of Acts, elders appear as responsible officials in Jerusalem (11:30). From that time onward they appear side by side with the apostles (15:2,4,6,22-23; 16:4) and were appointed in every church on the first missionary journey by Barnabas and Paul (14:23).

Individual churches in New Testament times had more than one elder (Acts 11:30; 20:17). This may be explained by the fact that members of the apostolic churches assembled in homes and other meeting places. It is entirely possible that a number of home churches or congregations made up one church. This probably corresponded to the plurality of elders in the synagogue.

In the Book of Acts, the elders are also described as tending the flock and exercising oversight. Paul said to the Ephesian elders: "For I did not shrink from declaring to you the whole counsel of God. Take heed to yourselves and to all the flock, in which the Holy Spirit has made you overseers [bishops], to care for the church of God which he obtained with the blood of his own Son" (20:27-28).

Bishop.—The first mention of the office of *bishop* in the New Testament is found in Acts 20:27-28. The Revised Standard Version translates the word as "overseer." There Paul told the Ephesian elders to "take heed to yourselves and to all the flock" (v. 28). The apostle wrote to the church at Philippi, "with the bishops and deacons" (1:1). Perhaps by this time the name "elder" had yielded to "bishop." In 1 Timothy 3:1-7 Paul spoke of the office of the bishop to which "if anyone aspires . . . he desires a noble task," and proceeded to lay down the qualifications for the office.

The Greek word for bishop *(episcopos)* literally means "overseer." In fact, overseer would be a more desirable translation because the modern word *bishop* connotes more than the New Testament usage intended. The term *elder* has a rich Jewish heritage and denotes a spiritual leader. The term *bishop,* derived from Greek usage, designates one who has the oversight of others.

In the new congregations elders were appointed as overseers in order to conserve the results of missionary preaching and to feed the flock of Christ (Acts 14:23; 20:27-28). In 1 Peter 2:25 Paul described Christ as the Shepherd (pastor) and Guardian (bishop) of your souls. Apparently these two titles are used interchangeably in the New Testament.

Pastor.–The title most commonly used today to describe the leader in the church is the one which is least used in the New Testament. In Ephesians 4:11 Paul described the gifts bestowed on the church by the ascended Christ. Included in this list were "some pastors and teachers, to equip the saints for the work of the ministry, for building up the body of Christ."

It is not difficult to see why this term has increased in favor. The term *pastor* still signifies what it was intended to mean in the New Testament writings. The other terms have taken on associations which imply more than the New Testament usage intended.

Furthermore, the shepherding style of ministry more nearly describes the ministry of Jesus while He was among us. Jesus was identified as "the good shepherd" (John 10:11) and "the great shepherd of the sheep" (Heb. 13:20). This described the caring, loving, affectionate oversight which the great Shepherd had over His flock. The risen Christ gave a threefold charge to Peter: "Feed my lambs," "Tend my sheep," and "Feed my sheep" (John 21:15-19). The admonition of Paul to the Ephesian elders "to feed the church of the Lord" has already been mentioned (Acts 20:28).

The word *pastor* means shepherd, and thus refers to the personal care and spiritual concern which the bishop-elder should exercise over his flock.

Summary.—It seems obvious that offices within the early church began to develop out of the distinct kinds of work or ministries the church began to do. This is not unlike the way our multiple staff ministries have developed within larger modern-day churches. It is not unusual for a church to have a senior minister (pastor) whose primary tasks are preaching and pastoral care, a church administrator (bishop) whose primary task is to oversee the business life of the church, and a minister of Christian education whose primary task is to equip the saints for their work in the ministry.

The form of ministry which is consistent with the essential character of the New Testament records is a ministry of "servants" recognized for the service they render rather than the position they occupy.

Deacons

The origin of the office of deacon is a good example of ministry arising out of the mission of the early church. A new task or need resulted in a new ministry or office. Though the term *deacon* does not occur in the passage, the circumstances recounted in Acts 6:1-6 probably describe the origin of the office. As the work of ministering to the needy began to demand more and more of the apostles' time, they sought out interested and qualified persons to assist them in a ministry of "helps." The contrast between "serve tables" and "the ministry of the word" was clearly defined (vv. 2,4).

The word *deacon (diaconos)* simply means servant and in that sense appears often in the New Testament. In two passages the term appeared in a more official sense. In the salutation to the church at Philippi, Paul wrote, "To all the saints in Christ Jesus . . . , with the bishops and deacons" (1:1). In 1 Timothy 3:8-13, the apostle gave the character and qualifications necessary for the office of deacon. However, deacons' duties were only intimated.

Two deacons (Philip and Stephen) preached, along with their other assignments. The servant model would allow a broad base of understanding of deacons' duties. From Acts 6:1-7 we learn that their duties included some understanding of the business life of the church, help in solving the distribution problem, and attention to some administrative detail.

Many interpreters point to two passages for evidence that female deacons existed in some apostolic churches. In Romans 16:1, where Paul spoke of Phoebe as a "deaconess of the church at Cenchreae," he used a form of the Greek word *diakonos*. The women whose qualifications were defined in 1 Timothy 3:11, are considered by some to be the wives of deacons. Others are convinced that the reference was to female officials or to women who were deacons. The question of the appointment of deaconesses was, doubtless, determined by each church for itself. Throughout church history ordination has been primarily in the hands of the local church.

Conclusion

For the sake of clarity, some conclusions concerning ministry in the New Testament church should be restated. First, there is evidence of progress in the organization of the Christian community. No consistent pattern of church life can be identified. Organization was dynamic, flexible.

Second, the recognition of essential ministries and the acceptance of new ministries were controlled by the church herself. This involved a process of discovering what the church was to do.

Third, as regular, ongoing ministries began to emerge, the persons responsible became "officers" of the church. Those servants of the church were recognized more by the service they rendered than by the office they occupied.

Finally, the structure of the early church varied and remained adaptable to the demands of the mission to be accomplished. A new task demanded a new ministry or office.

These ideas should be kept in mind as the modern-day church attempts to distinguish between temporary adjustments and time-less principles.

Note

1. See A. H. Strong, *Systematic Theology*, p. 901.

Bibliography

Conner, W. T. *Christian Doctrine*. Nashville: Broadman Press, 1937.

Dana, H. E. *A Manual of Ecclesiology*. Kansas City, Kan.: Central Sem-inary Press, 1944.

Dargan, Edwin C. *Ecclesiology: A Study of the Churches*. Louisville: Chas. T. Dearing, 1897.

Flew, R. Newton. *Jesus and His Church*. London: Epworth Press, 1938.

Guthrie, Donald. *New Testament Theology*. England: Inter-Varsity Press, 1981.

Harvey, H. *The Church: Its Polity and Ordinances*. Philadelphia: Ameri-can Baptist Publication Society, 1879.

Hinson, E. Glenn. *The Integrity of the Church*. Nashville: Broadman Press, 1978.

Ladd, George Eldon. *A Theology of the New Testament*. Grand Rapids, Mich.: Wm. B. Eerdmans Publishing Company, 1974.

Martin, Ralph P. *The Family and the Fellowship: New Testament Images of the Church*. Grand Rapids, Mich.: Wm. B. Eerdmans, 1980.

McCall, Duke K. *What Is the Church?* Nashville: Broadman Press, 1958.

McEachern, Alton H. *Set Apart for Service*. Nashville: Broadman Press, 1980.

Moody, Dale. *The Word of Truth*. Grand Rapids, Mich.: Wm. B. Eerdmans, 1981.

Review and Expositor, Vol. LXXVIII, No. 4 (Fall, 1981). Louisville: Southern Baptist Theological Seminary, 1981.

Strong, Augustus Hopkins. *Systematic Theology*. Fleming H. Revell Company, 1907.

Trueblood, Elton. *The Incendiary Fellowship*. New York: Harper & Row, 1967.

Watson, David. *I Believe in the Church*. Grand Rapids, Mich.: Wm. B. Eerdmans, 1978.

8
Types of Church Government

Every New Testament congregation of believers was somehow organized and governed. Yet, no single, consistent pattern of church organization emerged in the apostolic era. Through the years a variety of organization and government has developed, all claiming biblical authority. All Christian groups look to the same New Testament to find the roots of their polity. Each group finds language in the New Testament which seems to suggest its chosen form of polity.

What Is Polity?

In reference to religious denomination, polity is a system or method of organization by which a group of people choose to govern themselves or are governed.[1] Generally people do not drift toward cooperation and majority rule. Rather, the drift is toward centralization or control in the hands of the few.

Essential New Testament Concepts

As one traces the organizational development of the early church from "bud to blossom to fruit," certain essential concepts emerge. First, the New Testament church recognized the sole authority of Christ. "All authority in heaven and on earth has been given to me," Christ claimed (Matt. 28:18). Paul wrote, "Christ is the head of the church" and "the church is subject to Christ, . . . in everything" (Eph. 5:23-24). Acceptable church government must acknowledge the authority of Christ.

Second, the New Testament church recognized the right of the local church to govern itself under the lordship of Christ. In prescribing the treatment of private grievances, Christ advised His followers to "tell it to the church" (Matt. 18:17). The final appeal was to the church as a congregation. The word which describes this is *autonomy*. It means that each local church has the authority to develop its own program, call its own leadership (pastors and deacons), and be accountable to God for its decisions (Acts 20:28; Phil. 1:1).

Third, the New Testament church recognized the complete freedom of every Christian to respond to the authority of the lordship of Christ in matters of conscience. When Peter and the apostles were charged not to teach in the name of Jesus, they answered, "We must obey God rather than men" (Acts 5:29). Paul urged fellow believers, "Who are you to pass judgment on the servant of another? It is before his own master that he stands or falls. And he will be upheld, for the Master is able to make him stand" (Rom. 14:4). The individual Christian is not to be coerced by any individual or institution (Acts 24:10-16; 25:7-12).

A Summary Statement

The doctrine of the priesthood of all believers insists on the believer's right of direct access to God without any human or institutional mediator. It holds that each individual Christian is capable of dealing directly with God for himself.

Because Christians have an equal right of access to God, they are entitled to equal privileges in the church. Since each Christian is free to respond to the authority of Christ, the authority for deciding church matters should be located in the majority decisions of the assembled members (Acts 6:5; 2 Cor. 2:6; 1 Pet. 5:3; 3 John 9-10).

Jesus suggested that organization was necessary when He called his followers together and sent them out two-by-two (Mark 6:7-13). He gave them instructions for a specific assignment. He requested that they return to Him and report the results of their labors. Organization is suggested also in the mission of the seventy (Luke 10:1-24).

The development of government or polity within the early church was gradual and progressive. It was a system characterized by trial, error, and change. Every system that has developed since that time has strengths and weaknesses. The search for the "perfect" system continues.

The Big Three

Different forms of church polity or government have multiplied over the years. The shape of a particular denominational structure is determined largely by its organizer or the group to whom it is responsible. No two denominations are the same. The result is a variety of organization and government, all claiming biblical authority. However, three distinct forms have emerged as dominant: episcopal, presbyterial, and congregational.

Episcopal or Hierarchical

In the episcopal form of church government, the hierarchical idea is dominant. Ecclesiastical power belongs to a hierarchy of priests, usually called bishops. In the Roman Catholic Church, the pope is supreme bishop. The chief power resides in a self-perpetuating body, distinct from and virtually independent of the individual local congregation.

The episcopal system affirms that Christ gave supreme authority to Peter when He said, "And I tell you, you are Peter, and on this rock I will build my church, and the powers of death shall not prevail against it. I will give you the keys of the kingdom of heaven, and whatever you bind on earth shall be bound in heaven, and whatever you loose on earth shall be loosed in heaven" (Matt. 16:18-19). Then, by a process of continuous succession, authority has been transmitted to others.

Any denominational group where chief power resides in the clergy would be related in some way to the episcopal form of polity. Those who hold to other forms of church government insist that Peter's confession of Christ formed the rock upon which the church was built, not Peter himself. Further they insist that there was no evidence that Peter had any authority that was transmitted to others. Nor was there any evidence of continuous succession.

The hierarchical type of denominational structure has obvious advantages. It is probably the most efficient and economical. Authority flows quickly one way because control is in the hands of the few. Decisions are made at a higher level and are superimposed upon the local congregation. Day-to-day decisions can be made more quickly and smoothly.[2] However, even in the situation where the pastor tries to "run the church," numerous problems emerge. Church history has collected abundant evidence of corruption and misuse of power where control resides in the few.

Presbyterial or Delegated

In the presbyterial form of church government, the individual member delegates responsibility for the business operations of the church to an authoritative group. This group has been called by many names. In this system, the chief power resides in some subsidiary body with power to act in behalf of the congregation. They are elected by the individual congregation for that purpose. In essence they become a board of directors with power to act for the body.

This delegated type of structure has certain advantages. The most obvious is that individual members do not have to be bothered by business meetings or the day-to-day operations of the church or denomination. Also, there tends to be more unity and definiteness within a small group.

The inherent weaknesses are the same as in the episcopal system. Members play an observer, spectator role. They are not included in the planning of the activities they must ultimately promote. The observers often assume they know more than those who play the game. Spectators are often the greatest critics. The most serious weakness is that many people gifted with leadership potential have no arena in which to practice their skills. Once power has been delegated, it is difficult to ever regain it.[3]

Congregational or Democratic

In the congregational form of church government, all ecclesiastical power is exercised by each local church assembled as a congregation. Each separate congregation governs itself without reference to any higher organization. Each individual church holds its own business meetings or church conferences for the purpose of determining church policy. They aspire toward cooperation, unity, and majority rule.

In the New Testament are numerous indications in the early churches that the congregational form of government was used. The New Testament church recognized (1) the sole authority of Christ, (2) the right of the local church to govern itself under the lordship of Christ, and (3) the complete freedom of every Christian to respond to the authority of Christ in matters of conscience.

To these should be added further evidences: (1) Most of Paul's letters in the New Testament were addressed to churches (Rome, Corinth, Ephesus, and so on), not just to elected leadership or responsible delegates. The church as a whole was expected to hear the letter read and act accordingly. (2) There is evidence that the early churches elected their own leadership. In Acts 6:2-3 the twelve apostles called together the entire body of believers and said "pick out from among you seven men." (3) Apparently the entire assembly of the church had power to receive, discipline, and dismiss its members. In Acts 10:47 Peter referred the matter of accepting certain brethren for baptism by asking, "Can any one forbid water for baptizing these people?" In matters of church discipline, the final appeal of the aggrieved party was to the church as a congregation, not to elected leadership or representatives (Matt. 18:17; 1 Cor. 5:1-5; 2 Cor. 2:4-5). (4) The Great Commission and the ordinances were committed to the whole church to observe and guard (Matt. 28:19-20; 1 Cor. 11:2,

23-24). It seems evident that New Testament church government proceeded on the supposition that Christ dwells in all believers.[4]

Congregational polity is undergirded by two basic theological concepts: (1) the priesthood of every believer and (2) the autonomy of the local congregation. Once these theological beliefs are accepted, it follows that the conscience of the individual believer must not be violated nor the will of the individual congregation coerced. Therefore, the local body of believers will insist on a congregational form of government.

Congregational polity is not without its weaknesses. It can be expensive and often is slow to make changes. Local churches as well as denominational agencies chafe under the gradual decision-making process. Instantaneous reversals of direction are impossible. The meetings where issues are debated and individual opinions are expressed are misunderstood by those who practice other forms of government.

On the other hand, strength may develop out of these weaknesses. Congregational polity is dynamic and effective in carrying out the wishes of the majority. Each individual believer participates in the decision making process and, therefore, is more supportive of programs and objectives. The passing of time while waiting on the democratic process ensures calmer minds, opportunity for reevaluation, and greater continuity. Someone has said that a motorcycle can execute a U-turn more easily than a large truck. But, we all know which arrives with the cargo.

Other Forms

The three forms of church government mentioned above have emerged as dominant. However, other types of denominational organizations exist. Three will be considered here. Most major denominations will follow some variation of the six.

The Absence of Organization

One approach to church government would be to carefully preserve its absence. This type of denomination deliberately shuns all efforts toward formal structure. Emphasis on the deeper spiritual life and the leadership of the Holy Spirit results in a deemphasis on form, structure, and advance planning. The movement is away from congregational government because action is inspired either by one individual or by a small group.

The advantages of this approach are obvious. It appeals to many because it is thought to be a spiritual approach. It stresses the depth of Christian fellowship and Christlikeness in life-style. Also, it is appealing to those who are inherently suspicious of organization and are concerned about the high costs of denominational structures.

The weaknesses are obvious also. The total absence of denominational organization would mean that no program or project could be implemented which is larger than the group which conceived the idea. Such a denomination could not support worldwide mission efforts, build educational institutions or hospitals, or provide retirement benefits for employees.[5]

The Independent Organization

Another approach to church structure is the large, independent church which tends to become a minidenomination within itself. Even though these churches are highly organized within, they tend toward isolationaism from other organized bodies. More often than not, they will organize their own schools, send their own missionaries, and function as a denomination to themselves.

Generally these churches are led by strong, charismatic pastors who exercise a dominant leadership role. They tend toward an autocratic or authoritarian approach to church government. It is not uncommon for the pastor to hold deed and title to the church buildings, for the church to have no stated business meetings, and for the church staff to determine programs and procedures for the people.

Cooperation with other independent bodies would be out of the question because of the loss of control. Therefore, they select and send as missionary personnel only those whom they can personally supervise.

One can see immediately the advantages of this approach. An independent church can move quickly. It is not necessary to wait on committee action or anyone's approval. The organized body simply moves along lines predetermined by the strong personality and dynamic leadership of the pastor.

The basic weakness of this approach is also obvious. The continuity of leadership necessary in any movement is lacking. When a strong leader, who has built everything around himself, passes from the scene, it is not unusual to see his congregation diminish in size and influence.[6]

The Society System

This particular structure deals with how individual churches may relate to the denomination or more specifically to the agencies and institutions which carry out programs in their behalf. In this case, societies are formed to promote such things as missions, publications, and education. These become channels through which the churches combine and coordinate their work, but are not owned and controlled by the churches.

The primary strength of the society system is that various projects can be launched more quickly and, at times, more efficiently. It is not necessary to wait for denominational approval. Even projects of lesser importance require only a small group of interested people.

The weaknesses are many. The individual church tends to be bombarded by each separate society promoting its particular project. Each society is a separate entity. It is not accountable to the churches it represents. The possibility of conflict is ever present.

Another weakness is that the societies and the denomination they serve may grow farther and farther apart. Also, with the multiplication of societies, the problem of coordination and correlation becomes greater. It is difficult to harmonize efforts toward achieving common goals.[7]

Conclusion

The development of church polity or government was gradual and progressive. Polity is simply the system chosen by a group of believers by which they are governed. These number of systems or methods have grown through the years. The result is a variety of organizational patterns all claiming biblical authority. This leaves little room for dogmatism.

However, the weight of New Testament evidence seems to support some form of congregational polity. The individual Christian's right of direct access to God should entitle him or her to equal privileges in the church. Change is the only certainty. The search for the most functional system continues.

Notes

1. See James L. Sullivan, *Baptist Polity* (Nashville: Broadman Press, 1983), p. 51 *ff*.
2. Ibid., pp. 78-81.
3. Ibid., pp. 81-85.
4. Ibid., pp. 24-25.
5. Ibid., pp. 71-73.
6. Ibid., pp. 73-78.
7. Ibid., pp. 85-91.

Bibliography

Conner, W. T. *Christian Doctrine*. Nashville: Broadman Press, 1937.
Dargan, Edwin C. *Ecclesiology: A Study of the Churches* Louisville: Chas. T. Dearing, 1897.

Harvey, H. *The Church: Its Polity and Ordinances*. Philadelphia: American Baptist Publication Society, 1879.

Guthrie, Donald. *New Testament Theology*. England: Inter-Varsity Press, 1981.

McCall, Duke K. *What Is the Church?* Nashville: Broadman Press, 1958.

Strong, Augustus Hopkins. *Systematic Theology*. Fleming H. Revell Company, 1907.

Sullivan, James L. *Baptist Polity As I See It*. Nashville: Broadman Press, 1983.

9
Church Order

Christ and the church are inseparable realities. Christ did not leave the future of His work with individual, pious particles floating about. He left a body of believers, the church. To think of Christ is necessarily to think of the church. To think of the church is necessarily to think of Christ. The work of the church is Christ's work. Through the church, His purposes are carried out in the world.

In order to minister to the world in Christ's name, the church has developed structures. It is impossible to explore church officers and church government without reference to church order. On the one hand, there is no such thing as *the* New Testament order for the church. No order is so explicit in Scripture that it may be taken as a law to imitate. On the other hand, evidence abounds that the early church did structure itself for ministry.

In exploring the church's order, we are also attempting to understand the essential nature of the church. Since another book in this series is being written on that subject, this chapter will be brief.

Order in the Early Church

A careful study of the New Testament passages related to the early church reveals certain essentials or norms concerning church order. Many of these have been stated in previous chapters. A brief restatement of some of these biblical norms is necessary.

The Church Prior to Order

In the beginning the church had no formal structure. Primarily, it took on the form of a family gathered around Jesus. When Jesus called to Himself a group of followers, the result was the church in miniature.

The Earliest Evidences of Order

The church did not begin to take form until after the death and resurrection of Christ. The movement was from Christian fellowship to organized institution. Structure was the result of a growth process.

While Jesus was on earth, the new community was in embryonic form. The church was still vitally connected to the bodily presence of Christ. As their preacher-teacher, He was their reason for being.

After the death and resurrection of Christ, the church became the community of the risen Lord. The local congregations were made up of Christians who believed in the resurrection. They met for worship on "the first day of the week" as a constant reminder of their risen Lord (1 Cor. 16:2; Acts 20:7).

The Earliest Need for Order

The living presence of Christ in the form of the Holy Spirit is necessary to understanding the church. Acts 2 tells of the coming of the Holy Spirit into the church as transforming power. Many Christians trace the origin of the church as a self-conscious community to the Day of Pentecost. After that experience, those who were being baptized were added to the group (Acts 2:41,47).

After Pentecost the church faced a new situation which demanded some form of church order. How would the new power be harnessed and directed toward launching the church's worldwide mission? Unlimited power without structure or form could be dangerous. Apparently Paul discovered a situation where that problem existed and wrote about it in his first letter to the Corinthians.

Order Expressing Itself in Responsible Leadership

The twelve apostles emerged to bridge the gap between those who knew Jesus personally and the following generation. They filled a unique place as irreplaceable eyewitnesses. Their writings became our New Testament. They prepared the church for general and local officers necessary to the ongoing ministry.

Reading the New Testament, one can see the church take on dimension and life. There is undoubtedly development. New situations necessitated new forms of service. Churches living side by side adopted very different order. In those early years, organization was dynamic. For example, the house churches described in the Book of Acts reflect a loose, flexible structure.

However, from the beginning the church had leaders. More often than not the church chose as its leaders those people from whom it had repeatedly experienced authoritative guidance. Those chosen as officers had proved themselves.

The priesthood of all believers.—A constant theme in the New Testament is that the gift of grace is bestowed on every church member and that, therefore, every member is called to service (see Chapter 2). Every Christian is a priest or a minister and thus has a ministry to perform. The church's task is too great. No professional class of ministers or priests can do what the church is called to do.

Some called to specialized ministries.—As church life developed, the church began to do distinct kinds of work. Each separate congregation began to develop regular programs of worship, teaching, and service ministries. As these ministries began to crystallize into categories, the persons responsible became "officers" of the church (see Chapter 7).

Time passed and congregations grew. In time churches began to see that some of their ministry could be more effectively done by members who did not have to worry about their livelihood. One such officer was the pastor (bishop, elder). This officer was responsible for tending the flock and exercising oversight (Acts 20:27-28). He gave personal care and spiritual concern to overseeing the church.

The ascended Christ, in bestowing gifts on the church, gave "some pastors and teachers, to equip the saints for the work of ministry, for building up the body of Christ" (Eph. 4:11-12). The professional ministers were responsible for finding ways and means for each believer to share in the ministry to the whole community.

Order Expressing Itself in Discipleship and Discipline

The followers of Christ became known as disciples or learners. Discipleship refers to the quality of life the Christian is expected to live. Authentic discipleship involves careful and lifelong obedience to the teachings of Christ.

Discipline refers to the corrective or reformative measures that are sometimes necessary for the Christian in relationship to the church (1 Cor. 5:1-13; 2 Cor. 2:5-11; Matt. 18:15-18). Apparently the early church was structured to practice corrective discipline. The motive for such discipline was remedial, not vengeful. The principle of discipline within the life of Christian discipleship remains a valid teaching of the New Testament (see Chapter 3).

Order Expressing Itself in Worship and Ordinances

The New Testament church began immediately to structure itself for worship and for the continuing practice of baptism and the Lord's Supper. Worship was a teaching drama reenacting what God had done in Christ's incarnation and resurrection. Christ had promised His presence when they gathered in His name (Matt. 18:20), therefore believers were urged not to neglect to meet together (Heb. 10:25).

Worship became recognized as the meeting between God and His people. It was essential to the ongoing life of the church. According to Luke, the early Christians "devoted themselves to the apostles' teaching and fellowship, to the breaking of bread and the prayers" (Acts 2:42). Concerning structures for worship, Paul urged that "all things should be done decently and in order" (1 Cor. 14:40) (see Chapters 4 and 5).

Also, Jesus retained two ceremonial ordinances for perpetual observance. So, as the church structured itself for worship, it made provision for the ongoing observance of baptism and the Lord's Supper. These great teaching dramas were instituted to provide an authentic memory of the heart of the gospel—resurrection and atonement (see Chapter 6).

Order Expressing Itself in Evangelism and Missions

Early in the life of the church, believers realized that form and structure would be necessary on a wider basis than just the local church. Christ's commission was clearly "to all nations" (Matt. 28:19; Luke 24:47) and "to the end of the earth" (Acts 1:8). Form could not end with the local church.

Acts 15 shows that the early churches were not entirely separated from one another. The Jerusalem Council was made up of representatives from individual churches who had been called together in a time of real crisis. There was a meeting, a moderator, an appeal to Scripture, and a satisfactory solution. All this reflects a form or structure wider than the local church.

The family of faith shares the essential task of evangelizing all who profess no personal relationship to Jesus Christ and enlisting unaffiliated Christians for effective service. The universal mission of the church has dimensions which are local, regional, national, and international.

The church at Antioch (Acts 13) felt compelled to respond to the challenge of the risen Christ: "You shall be my witnesses . . . to the end of the earth" (Acts 1:8). Luke recorded their action: "While they were worshiping the Lord and fasting, the Holy Spirit said, 'Set apart for me Barnabas and Saul for the work to which I have called them.' Then after fasting and praying they laid their hands on them and sent them off" (Acts 13:2-3). From that time on, the church found it necessary to form itself for a worldwide ministry.

Church Order and Freedom

The church must have an ordered ministry. The foregoing essentials or biblical norms reflect the types of form already being developed in the New Testament church. Some of these principles are timeless and should guide the organized church in the twentieth century as well as any other century. On the other hand, it is obvious that some structures in the early church were spontaneous and remained adaptable to the demands of the mission.

Form and Freedom

Early Christianity spread chiefly through the planting of churches. The apostle Paul established churches in the different cities he visited as a missionary. The structures of these early churches varied. Some were organized like the Jewish synagogue because all the members were recently converted Jews. The church in Jerusalem reflected a different structure from the one in Corinth.

Generally speaking, the primitive church emphasized its different nature with surprising freedom by creating new ministries and transforming old ones. While certain forms were commanded by God, vast areas were left free. In the New Testament church there is both form and freedom.

Christian liberty is always freedom within bounds. The New Testament sets the boundary conditions for form within the church. However, within these boundary conditions, believers have the freedom to be adaptable and spontaneous under the leadership of the Holy Spirit for particular times and places. In a rapidly changing age like the present, to make nonabsolutes into absolutes may create havoc for the church.

An Illustration of Form and Freedom

New Testament church order expressed itself in the choosing of responsible leadership. Some leaders were called to specialized ministries and became officers of the church. Christian ministry became their vocation, and they were supported by the churches.

However, other ministries were encouraged and often were performed, not by professional clergy but by spiritually gifted church members. The New Testament does not give a distinct picture of these ministries. In fact, four lists of spiritual gifts are recorded in the New Testament, and each list is different.

The longest list is recorded in 1 Corinthians 12:8-10 and gives nine spiritual gifts: the utterance of wisdom, the utterance of knowledge, faith, gifts of healing, working of miracles, prophecy, the ability to distinguish between spirits, various kinds of tongues, and interpretation of tongues. The list is not intended to be complete or exhaustive; it is representative. Later in the same chapter Paul gave another list which includes eight spiritual gifts. He added two new ministries which are not included elsewhere: helpers and administrators (see 1 Cor. 12:28-30).

Another list of seven gifts appeared in Romans 12:6-8. This list included four new functions which have a new relevance: exhortation (encouragement), liberality, giving aid, and acts of mercy.

A fourth list is found in Ephesians 4:11 and adds two new ministries: evangelists and pastors (shepherds).

To classify these gifts would be difficult if not impossible. The order is different in each case. New ministries are introduced in each list. Obviously, Paul was not outlining an existing hierarchy of neatly separated orders. Rather he was simply illustrating the plurality and unity of the ministries of the church. Also he was acknowledging the sovereignty of the Spirit "who apportions to each one individually as he wills" (1 Cor. 12.11).

It is a good thing that scholars have not been able to agree on the exact pattern that the ministry actually had in the first century.

This favors spontaneity over formality. It emphasizes the freedom of the Spirit at work within the recognizable forms or structures of the early church.

Some Guidelines for Adapting Form and Structure

How can the church remain open both to the revealed order of the New Testament and to the freedom of the Spirit's leadership? Eduard Schweizer has suggested three ways in which church order can remain open to God's active intervention:

> First, it can be broken through by God's giving an instruction to an otherwise uncommissioned church member (1 Cor. 14:30; cf. Acts 11:27-30). Secondly, God's initiative creates new ministries not hitherto forseen (Acts 13:1-3). This, of course, is true not merely in direct revelations by the Spirit, but equally so when the church listens to God as it confronts a new situation (Acts 6:1ff.), or when a new ministry is at first simply carried out on someone's own initiative and is recognized afterwards by the church (1 Cor. 16:16). Thirdly, however, it is also possible that certain ministries have proved their worth and are being continued, but that the church tries seriously later on to find out who has received from God the gifts of grace that are necessary for them (1 Tim. 3:1ff.).[1]

To avoid inpulsive changes the church should consider certain guidelines in adapting form and structure:

1. Realize that, even though the church has a definite order, it must be always open to amendment. Where God reveals a clearly different way, non-absolutes must never become absolutes.

2. Every church member had responsibility to minister by means of his or her particular gift. "To each is given the manifestation of the Spirit *for the common good*" (1 Cor. 12:7, author's italics). Spiritual gifts are not personal merit badges to mark the level of achievement. Rather, they are devinely distributed powers intended for the benefit of the entire congregation.

3. The church must decide the limits of its ministry on the basis of the gifts of grace God has bestowed on its members. The modern-day church tends to reverse this order. The temptation is

to predetermine the nature of the ministry, then look for the spiritually gifted people.

4. Survey the needs of the community in which the church is located. Each community will present unique social, economic, health, family, and educational conditions to which the church must minister.

5. Project certain objectives in church ministry which relate to the particular situation. Strike a balance in the worship, evangelism, education, social, world-wide ministries of the church.

6. The church's ministry is a very personal one. Many of the forms and structures of the past still have merit. They are not to be supplanted by gimmicks and slick programs. Be willing to experiment with new forms and structures in situations which call for new ministries.

7. Larger congregations must be divided into smaller units for purposes of service and ministry. Nothing has ever taken the place of the fellowship and individualized ministry of the Sunday School class in the larger chruch.[2]

The Church Ordered for Ministry in Today's World

The church is different from the world, yet it exists for the sake of the world. The church offers programs within the church, yet has ministries which are outside the church. The church must exist in the world, yet, it must exist, at the same time, apart from the world. This is both the paradox and the miracle of the church.

Where Is the Church on Sunday?

The church is ordered for stated times of worship, Bible study, training, mission study, and outreach. This represents the church gathered. These programs are offered at stated hours at the church house. They represent the "come" structures of the church. Jesus did say, "Come to me, . . . and I will give you rest" (Matt. 11:28).

These are necessary times if Christians intend to sustain vital experiences with Christ. During the times of assembly, we come to know the Lord better; we come to a better understanding of the

Christian life; and we encourage one another to be faithful. The stated times of coming together are necessary to the total Christian enterprise. Unless we gather for worship there is no available power for witness in the world.

Where Is the Church on Monday?

The church must be so ordered that people will be thrust back out into the world for service. This pictures the church scattered. These programs represent the "go" structures of the church. Also Jesus said, "Go therefore and make disciples of all nations" (Matt. 28:19).

Just as it is important for believers to come together for corporate worship and serious study, it is also important that they be motivated for serving people in the world. During the week individual Christians must go out into all their worlds communicating the good news. The church's primary ministry is not in the church building but in the world.[3]

On Monday the church is where Christians are: on the job, at home with family, in leisure hours, at school, or on the athletic field. This creative tension between come and go is normal in the Christian life. It is a necessary part of the challenge and excitement of following Christ.

Notes

1. Eduard Schweizer, *Church Order in the New Testament*, p. 205.
2. See Ibid., pp. 228-229 and E. Glenn Hinson, *The Integrity of the Church*, pp. 111-13.
3. See Findley B. Edge, *The Greening of the Church*, p. 163-6.

Bibliography

Edge, Findley B. *The Greening of the Church*. Waco: Word Books, 1971.

Hinson, E. Glenn. *The Integrity of the Church*. Nashville: Broadman Press, 1978.

Minear, Paul. *Images of the Church in the New Testament*. Philadelphia: Westminster Press, 1960.

Raines, Robert A. *New Life in the Church*. New York: Harper & Row, 1961.

Schweizer, Eduard. *Church Order in the New Testament*. London: SCM Press, LTD., 1961.

Trueblood, Elton. *The Incendiary Fellowship*. New York: Harper & Row, 1967.

Watson, David. *I Believe in the Church*. Grand Rapids, Mich.: Wm. B. Eerdmans, 1978.

Scripture Index

150